THE NEVER COLD CALL AGAIN ONLINE PLAYBOOK

THE NEVER COLD CALL AGAIN ONLINE PLAYBOOK

The Definitive Guide to Internet Marketing Success

FRANK J. RUMBAUSKAS, Jr.

WILEY

John Wiley & Sons, Inc.

Published by John Wiley & Sons, Inc., Hoboken, New Jersey.
Published simultaneously in Canada.

For general information on our other products and services or for technical support, please contact our Customer Care Department within the United States at (800) 762-2974, outside the United States at (317) 572-3993 or fax (317) 572-4002.

Wiley also publishes its books in a variety of electronic formats. Some content that appears in print may not be available in electronic books. For more information about Wiley products, visit our web site at www.wiley.com.

Library of Congress Cataloging-in-Publication Data:

Rumbauskas, Frank J., 1973–
   The never cold call again online playbook : the definitive guide to internet marketing success / Frank J. Rumbauskas, Jr.
      p. cm.
   ISBN 978-0-470-50392-8 (pbk.)
   1. Internet marketing.   I. Title.
   HF5415.1265.R86 2009
   658.8'72–dc22

                                                        2009027774

Printed in the United States of America

10 9 8 7 6 5 4 3 2 1

To John Galt and the vision of Ayn Rand

CONTENTS

FOREWORD

Armando Montelongo
America's Top Real Estate Investor

If you are wondering if this is the right book for you, remember the term "Floppy Mop" and then read on . . .

In Internet marketing, there are three types of people: The "student" who is willing and eager to learn; the "mentor" who pretends to be successful in order to get the "student" to order their info products; and the very few and very far between—the "Master."

The Master is someone who walks his talk, makes money in the business, and then, one day, has made so much money he decides to contribute outside himself because he genuinely likes helping people. And more money won't make a difference in the quality of his life.

Frank Rumbauskas is *that* MASTER!

I met Frank two years ago at an Internet marketing event in New York, and we hit it off like gangbusters. When you first meet Frank he doesn't tell you he is a *New York Times* bestseller (*Never Cold Call Again*, John Wiley & Sons, Inc.); he doesn't tell you that he makes six figures online in any given month; nor does he tell you he travels the world commanding huge audiences wanting his knowledge. Frank will simply ask you what you do and how do you want to improve on it.

It's that humility that makes him a marketer of the people and ultimately has created his success and wealth.

Let me explain. Most business models, especially in the personal development genre, are as follows: Give the people little of what they need so they always ask for more. In my opinion, this is because most "gurus" or "mentors" do not "walk their talk." They don't actually *do* the business, so how the hell could they teach a beginner how to make $10,000 in their first month of business?

However, there are more than a few things a Master will know and will ultimately be able to translate to his or her students, thus making them richer, faster. This was shown to me when Frank and his fiancée Dana went on a cruise last January with myself and my wife Veronica.

We were on our way to St. Thomas to bask in the sun (and have a margarita on the beach), and I asked Frank what he thought the key to his Internet success was. The answer was nothing of what I expected.

He told me of how you must first have a true business platform (which he will teach you) as the basis of your success. Then, you must be able to label or brand yourself from that point. This is where the conversation took an unexpected turn. Frank said that anybody can create a brand by simply looking at their uniqueness in a day-to-day format and then learn how to market themselves, what they are good at, or something they use that is basic and simple. For example, take the woman who created the Floppy Mop. She is a housewife who needed a better mop for everyday use. She created a platform, a brand, and then applied marketing and created a $600 million empire!

The amazing thing is that with the power of the Internet, it is possible to create a platform, brand, and market in half the time of television, with no risk or cost, and build an even bigger business!

Frank mentioned that every successful business must have these three elements for success. He told me if I evaluated my own businesses I would find that this holds true. I did and IT DOES.

What else would explain how Frank can send a single e-mail and make tens of thousands of dollars? It is because he has a platform, a brand, and an Internet marketing machine, and he will show you how to implement this in your new or existing business throughout the pages of this book.

PREFACE

Congratulations!

You now have in your hands the first complete guide to Internet marketing success that's available for only two figures.

This book contains more knowledge and education on Internet marketing than most home study courses costing $1,000, $2,000, or more. And believe me, if I were to put all of this information into a $2,000 course, it would sell.

I will reveal to you some of my very own marketing secrets that I swore I'd never give away when I began writing the book.

I'm going to explain to you, step-by-step, the exact process I used to start my Internet business with literally nothing, and achieve the immense success I enjoy today.

However, there's a catch.

Even though I'll tell you anything and everything you need to become a millionaire online, many of the examples and concepts are much easier to understand when you can physically *see* them. So, with that in mind, the online accompaniment to this book can be found at:

NeverColdCallBook.com

With that out of the way, I want to explain to you exactly what Internet marketing is.

Many people believe that Internet marketing refers solely to the "Internet marketing community," a large group—some call it an "underground"—of people who sell products online and who are very close-knit and regularly meet up at live events. They do joint ventures, promotions, and seminars, and discuss marketing daily in online forums.

The problem, though, is that the Internet marketing community is commonly believed to be a bunch of people who sell products solely on the topic of Internet marketing to each other, and who have no market or reach outside the Internet marketing community.

I'm sorry to report to you that this isn't the case.

While it may have been true to a degree at some point—it was in fact my first impression when I first came to Internet marketing in 2003—the reality is that while a core group exists who do indeed only sell products on the topic of Internet marketing, most of us are running regular, "offline" businesses, that simply harness the power of the Internet to make us a big bundle of money.

And what about those guys who only sell products directly related to Internet marketing?

Trust me, they're not selling them to each other. That would not be a sustainable business model! Instead, they're selling those products all over the world, in large volume, and making millions upon millions of dollars for themselves in the process.

And guess what—I'm one of the people who buys those products. An integral part of becoming a great marketer is to never stop learning.

No, Internet marketing is not some underground of creepy nerds who sit around selling the same stuff back and forth to each other.

It's mainstream.

It's cutting-edge.

It's the way business is done today, particularly if you want to become wealthy.

And the best part?

It's easy.

Whether you are a salesperson looking for leads, a small business owner who wants to promote on the Internet, a big corporation looking to expand your market, or an entrepreneur who wants to become a self-made millionaire, Internet marketing can do all of the above, and more, relatively easily.

It provides more power, more tools, more ability to test and measure, and exponential growth than were ever possible before.

It gave me, a salesman who was sick of working for someone else, the ability to put all of my sales knowledge on paper, put up a web site promoting it, and immediately begin selling so many copies of it online that I quit my last job ever only six weeks later, and have been free from work ever since.

It has given many people I know personally, many of them only in their twenties, the ability to become millionaires in a very short period of time.

What will it do for you?

Anything you want it to.

If you're an eager entrepreneur looking to make millions of dollars, welcome—you're home.

If you're a salesperson who wants to explode your sales results with the power of the Internet, or even start another business entirely and become free from a job, you've come to the right place.

If you're a small or large business that wants to grow exponentially, you're on the right track as well.

Internet marketing will do all of the above, and so much more.

Take notes as you read the book. If I ask you to do something at the end of a chapter, put the book down and do it. Also, be sure to check out the bonus materials for every chapter located at NeverColdCallBook.com.

And, most importantly of all, think big. Whatever your goal is now, double it, because the Internet has the power to achieve it!

ACKNOWLEDGMENTS

Anyone who has ever written a successful book knows that many people are involved in making it happen, and I want to thank everyone involved with this book.

First and most important, my lovely bride Dana, who was completely understanding when I needed to spend long hours alone in my office, or came home late at night, when I was getting this book done. I know many people who don't have such understanding at home. I'm so very thankful for Dana. You are the best!

Also to my family, who are so proud of my success, and who are always there for me, as I am for them.

To Dan Ambrosio, Matt Holt, and the staff at John Wiley & Sons, Inc., who not only published my very first book but also gave me fantastic feedback and input on this one, taking it from basic concept to the finished product. To all of my friends in the marketing world, thank you! I've learned more from you guys than I ever thought possible. There are far too many to mention here, but in no particular order, a ton of thanks go to Tom Beal, Mike Filsaime, Russell Brunson, Joel Therien, Armando Montelongo, Simon Leung, Deb and JP Micek, Dave Woodward, Dave Lakhani, Michael Port, Ross Goldberg, and many others.

Finally, I owe much gratitude to my readers, my customers, and all of my followers. I truly appreciate your ongoing support, and I look forward to continuing to help you achieve all of your goals, no matter how lofty they may be!

Part I

ONLINE
MARKETING TODAY

Everything You Know About Internet Marketing Is Probably Wrong

Ah, Internet marketing.

Most people who aren't Internet marketers themselves have absolutely no idea of what it's all about.

The greater problem, though, is that many of those who are in fact marketing on the Internet—or trying to, anyway—don't get it, either. They have false expectations about what's required to succeed online, and, on the flip side, they have no idea of just what one can achieve with the Internet, nor do they have the specialized knowledge to utilize it.

Let's begin with the former.

Many people who don't have any actual experience in selling or marketing anything on the Internet erroneously assume that it's a lot simpler than it really is. You have no idea of how much frustration I experience in working with people who have fantastic ideas for products, services, and more—along with some really bad ideas—but who are under the assumption that all it takes is a nice web site with an order button to rake in millions of dollars.

Nothing could be further from the truth.

I have encountered so many people who hear about Internet success stories and suddenly they're pushing to get a web site built and get it online. Many come to me, mostly looking for advice, but now and then someone will try to get me involved in a joint venture or partnership where I'd be doing the actual marketing.

They want to split the profits fifty-fifty, but they have *no idea* that as the marketer, I'd be doing the bulk of the work.

Don't let this scare you. Becoming successful at marketing on the Internet is not going to ruin your lifestyle or stick you with a 100-hour workweek. Not if you do it right, anyway—although plenty of successful marketers are working their tails off day and night, making "successful" a dubious term. As a successful Internet marketer, my Internet businesses now run on autopilot. I rarely ever have to do anything, freeing my time for enjoying life and recreational activities, and for projects like this book that would have never been possible had I been busy managing and maintaining my online businesses.

I built my first Internet business from scratch, with almost no money, and now, six years later, I'm living the lifestyle I've always dreamed of. I even utilized Internet marketing strategies to make my first published book, *Never Cold Call Again* (John Wiley & Sons, Inc., 2006) a *New York Times* bestseller, which has paid off big in many ways and elevated my success to a whole new level.

Of course, it's my leisurely lifestyle that creates the impression that reaching this level of success was quick and easy. That's not the way it was! But I will admit that it wasn't very difficult once I'd learned how to do it, but it definitely took time. You're not going to get instant results overnight, but you'll definitely get results—big results, if and only if you're willing to learn and execute.

The myth that all you need are a web site and a few simple tricks to succeed online has unfortunately spawned an entire cottage industry of get-rich-quick information products, some costing thousands of dollars, promising fast and easy Internet riches.

True, there are some high-quality information products out there. You can pick those out easily because they don't promise instant overnight success, and their authors are constantly driving home the fact that they had to put in time and effort to get things rolling before the cash came pouring in. Lots of good people are putting out quality Internet marketing products and courses, but for every good one there are a dozen hucksters trying to get your money. Beware!

Now, having given you fair warning that you're not going to become an instant overnight billionaire online (although you can certainly become a millionaire if you're willing to work at it), let's address the other half: people who are in fact marketing online, or more accurately, trying, but not getting the results they expected.

The reasons for not getting results can be any or all of the following:

- Assuming Internet marketing would guarantee fast and easy riches.
- Not staying up-to-date on current Internet marketing strategies.
- Not being willing to put in the work.
- Getting ripped off by an unqualified consultant or a huckster pushing get-rich-quick products.
- Marketing to the wrong markets online.
- Not controlling advertising costs.
- Being unwilling or uninformed about testing and optimizing various web pages, web site structures, and so on.
- Not maintaining a proper automated follow-up system.
- Writing poor web site copy.

Having said all that, many people do actually succeed online. Many thousands have changed their lives forever by successfully marketing on the Internet. I know, because I'm one of those people. I know dozens of Internet millionaires, and I've met hundreds of them at seminars, conferences, and other events.

Keep in mind that many people who will read this book are not fledgling entrepreneurs looking to get rich on the Internet. Many of you are salespeople. Sales managers. Marketing directors. Executives. And this book applies to all of you.

Whether you're a salesperson who has learned some Internet marketing strategies from my previous books and wants to learn more, or a sales manager looking to use the Internet to automate lead generation and follow-up, or a small business owner wanting to double or triple your income, you will find the answers you are looking for, as long as you remember that there is no such thing as get-rich-quick in the real world. But if you put in the time and effort to learn, apply what you have learned, and gain experience, you can easily use your newfound expertise to become an Internet millionaire yourself and succeed at anything you want!

2

YOUR INTERNET MARKETING GOALS

Internet marketing today has come a long way. It's no longer just about getting someone to your web site and hoping they'll order something online or pick up the phone. There are different goals for different people, such as:

- A salesperson may want to generate leads via the Internet in order to eliminate cold calling, while handling the rest of the sales process with traditional face-to-face appointments.
- A small business owner may want to generate leads in much the same fashion as a salesperson in order to free up the owner's time to do what he does best—servicing customers.
- An independent professional such as an attorney or accountant, who has no sales ability nor does he want to learn sales, may want to attract new high-quality clients via the Internet.
- A prospective author may want to use the Internet to sell an e-book online and develop that initial success into something much larger, as I have done.
- A musician or band may want to get exposure on the Internet in order to gain a following and be discovered by a major record label.

- A concerned citizen may want to use the Internet to further a political agenda.
- A budding entrepreneur may want to achieve her dream of becoming financially free and never having to work for someone else again.

As to Internet marketing strategy itself, it's no longer about simply getting someone to a web site and hoping they'll buy. Here is a nonexhaustive list of current Internet marketing strategies. Most or all of these will be utilized by a highly successful Internet marketer.

- Traffic generation
- E-mail marketing
- Lead capture and follow-up
- Product creation
- Building credibility
- Getting press and publicity
- Building buzz around you and/or your product(s)
- Podcasting
- Online video
- Blogging
- Using social media
- Tweeting
- Creating expert status
- Building a loyal following
- Writing effective sales copy
- Affiliate marketing
- Joint ventures
- Viral marketing
- Contests
- High-volume product launch strategy
- Membership sites
- Recurring continuity products
- Web site structure
- Increasing conversion rate
- Up-sells, cross-sells, and down-sells

- Testing and tracking
- Pay-per-click marketing
- Cost-per-action marketing
- Back-end products

I just wrote this list from memory because, with only one exception, I use all of these strategies—and more!

Depending on who you are and what you want to achieve, you may use all or only a few of these techniques. A salesperson who works for a corporation and simply wants to generate leads without cold calling is going to need only about half of the techniques in the preceding list. Someone like myself, however, who wants to make huge amounts of money on autopilot, is going to use everything you see there plus much more.

On the other hand, salespeople who are out to generate leads and nothing more will be surprised at how much of this list will apply to them. Just because you're not a business owner yourself doesn't mean you can't use the same powerful tools they do!

Yes, there is a lot to learn. Yes, it will take time.

Don't let that scare you, however. I don't work too hard these days unless I want to. The work is really only needed up-front, after which you can let your business run on autopilot and simply enjoy the income, with a minimal amount of tweaking maintenance work as needed. You can even outsource the bulk of that activity inexpensively and never have to think about it.

The other heads-up I need to give you is that Internet marketing is constantly changing. As you almost certainly know, there are new ways to market online appearing almost daily. A year ago few people had heard of Twitter, for example, but now it's becoming very popular and is a favorite of Internet marketers all over the world.

Before moving on to the next chapter, please put this book down for a few minutes and decide what your Internet marketing goals are. Write them down. Make them specific. Don't say, "I want to stop cold calling." Make your aim big and particular, like achieving

300 percent of your quota without cold calling. Don't say you want to get rich on the Internet. Again, make the goal specific: Decide on an exact amount of money you hope to acquire, and describe your ideal lifestyle, car, home, and toys too.

As my friend Joe Vitale likes to say, choose a specific goal. Then double it. Think big!

3

THE FUTURE OF INTERNET MARKETING

I've pointed out that Internet marketing is constantly changing. You need to stay on top of things, become friends with and create mastermind groups with other marketers, read or participate in online marketing forums, subscribe to valuable Internet marketing newsletters, and more.

There is one absolutely certain guarantee in the world of Internet marketing: It will always change, and if you don't keep up with the changes, your business will suffer and you won't succeed.

Ten years ago, few people could imagine that buying products online would become so common that it would eat away at the market share and profitability of many brick-and-mortar businesses, to such an extent that many are enduring financial hardship now.

Seven years ago, I had no idea I'd become financially free and never have to hold a job or own a traditional business again because of Internet marketing. I knew beyond a shadow of a doubt that I would achieve that goal, but I did not dream that it would happen so quickly and entirely because of the Internet. I'd always imagined myself working for at least ten years building a traditional offline business, with no idea of what that business might be.

Five years ago, the concept of social networking and social media was practically unheard of. I certainly would never have predicted that I'd become reunited with countless high school friends who are now living all over the country, and that I'd be logging into my social network accounts almost daily to keep in touch with everyone.

Two years ago I'd never heard of Twitter, yet today I use it daily on my iPhone no matter where I happen to be.

One year ago, nobody expected a young and relatively inexperienced candidate for President of the United States to break fundraising records through smart utilization of the Internet and go on to win the election, while his older opponent largely ignored the Internet, unaware of its power.

Today, I continue to be amazed at the massive opportunity that lies within the power of the Internet. Literally anyone can become wealthy and financially free with Internet marketing. That opportunity becomes larger and more accessible with each passing day as more and more tools are added to make the most of it.

For example, I began using Google AdWords pay-per-click marketing right from the start of my first Internet business (if you don't know what that is, don't worry, it will be covered in a subsequent chapter). Since then, Google AdWords has grown enormously. It has spread from simply showing ads in Google search results to serving ads on hundreds of major web sites like Amazon.com. Then Google introduced Gmail which has become incredibly popular (I use it myself). Google added AdWords ads to the Gmail interface, and millions of Gmail users now see those ads every time they use e-mail.

Twitter is another example. Now that it's becoming practically ubiquitous and millions of people, plus countless media outlets, use it daily, rumor has it that Twitter will soon feature inexpensive advertising, giving people like us access to millions of new potential customers.

Not too long ago it took prohibitively expensive equipment and software to record and display very high-quality video on a web site, but now it can be done easily and inexpensively with a cheap consumer camcorder.

Traffic generation and search engine optimization used to be a chore but now with free tools like social bookmarking, one can achieve relatively high search engine rankings—and the traffic that comes along with them—easily and at no cost.

Having your own radio show used to be practically unachievable for anyone who isn't famous or well-connected, but now anyone can record and upload a podcast to directories such as iTunes where millions of potential customers can find it—for free or at extremely low cost. Apple now includes professional-grade podcasting software, free, preloaded on every Mac computer!

Networking is on a whole new level now, and it has allowed me to grow my business beyond my wildest dreams. Thanks to free tools like Twitter and Facebook, I've made valuable contacts and even friends with many big-name people who were previously inaccessible, including extremely well-known authors, television stars, and media figures.

Speaking of media, I've been interviewed, quoted, or featured in countless media outlets, not because I'm some big-shot best-selling author, but because the Internet makes it easy to find those opportunities. I don't get media attention because I'm a best-selling author. Quite the contrary—I became a best-selling author, in part, by learning how to find media opportunities online.

I'm telling you all this in order to open your mind to the immense possibilities that the future of Internet marketing will hold for us all. Everything I've discussed in this chapter either didn't exist or was prohibitively difficult in just the recent past.

How many things that are impossible today will be free and easy tomorrow, all thanks to the Internet?

What amazing tools, strategies, and systems will pop up in the next six months that will enable us to reach an even greater audience—effectively—and promote our products and services to them?

My good friend Armando Montelongo, star of A&E Network's *Flip This House*, points out that getting a lead role on a reality show like *Flip This House* is not luck. There are proven formulas one can follow to make that happen, and building a solid foundation on the Internet is a key part of it.

When people ask me how to become a published author, I explain that the old routine of mailing out a manuscript and hoping a publisher likes it is just that—old. Today, you exploit highly effective Internet marketing strategies, use them to build a following, and then you present your results to the publisher along with your book proposal. If you don't have a strong Internet foundation, your odds of getting published are slim to none, but with a solid foundation online, you can even get book deals signed before the publisher sees your book!

These are just two examples. None of us can predict what the future of Internet marketing will hold, but I can tell you that it keeps getting better and better, and the opportunities ever greater.

4

MY SYSTEM OF SYSTEMS FOR MASSIVE ONLINE SUCCESS

Contrary to popular belief, successful Internet marketing is not about a jumble of different techniques and employing all of them randomly in order to succeed.

Traffic generation, viral marketing, copywriting, mechanisms and scripts to increase conversion rate—all of those things are important and will get you plenty of sales—but they won't give you access to the Internet's full potential.

I've achieved huge success online not by employing every trick in the book, but by doing so in a systematic, orderly fashion.

Every great Internet marketer understands the process I'm about to explain, and uses it to maximum potential. Before I discovered most of this process through a few years of my own trial-and-error experience, I first saw it explained by Mike Filsaime in his legendary Butterfly Marketing Manuscript (BMManuscript.com).

Here's a brief rundown of the marketing funnel I employ in my online businesses.

- Get prospective customers to my web site through a variety of techniques: search engine optimization, pay-per-click advertising, article marketing, PR and media coverage, social networking, affiliates, joint ventures, and much more.
- Get the visitor to opt-in (sign up) for my e-mail newsletter. Note: Please remember, throughout this book, that your *first and foremost* goal is to capture a lead! Every experienced marketer knows that "the money is in the list," and more important, in your relationship with that list. Internet marketing newcomers frequently assume that your goal in sending traffic to your site is to make a sale, but that's not true. Sure, you definitely want to make a sale as quickly as possible—depending on your product or service, the price, and the sales cycle—but even more important, you want to build long-term loyalty and years of sales to happy customers, not just a one-time hit.
- Viral marketing. After getting someone to sign up for my newsletter, I then ask him to tell his friends, in exchange for several free gifts, as his incentive to do so. (These free gifts are all downloadable media such as .pdf reports, MP3 audio files, video downloads, and so on, costing me nothing to distribute.) I use software (ViralMaximizer.com) that allows people to send a referral e-mail to their entire address book, if they so choose, maximizing my exposure and viral "copulation rate" (to be explained in a future chapter). Of course, visitors are free to skip this step, or to invite as few or as many friends as they'd like.
- Sales page. This is the heart of it all—the "sales letter" where the actual product is presented and sold to the customer. For those of you who have always assumed that the purpose of a web site is to get someone to buy right away or to pick up the phone and call you, look at all the steps that the prospective customer went through before ever seeing my sales page. That's the difference between someone who makes a living on the Internet and someone who becomes wealthy from it:

understanding that the secret to Internet millions is to maximize the value of every site visitor before trying to sell him or her something.

- Copywriting, testing, pricing, structure, and more. These are just some of the many components that go into creating a highly effective sales page, and you have no idea how much the tiniest changes can improve your sales results. This is all done, of course, with advanced testing and tracking software. Testing is a science all by itself—in fact, many of the advanced testing strategies I use today were developed by brilliant mathematicians—and is nowhere near as simple as "A vs. B."

- Shopping cart design and structure. This is a part of Internet marketing that, like sales pages, is largely misunderstood. Have you ever clicked the "Order Now" link below a product and been presented with a "You Must Register First" page? I have many times, and almost every time I click my back button and find someone else to buy from. This is just one example of how marketers are shooting themselves in the foot by using widely available shopping cart software and not realizing how much the bad design is hurting their business. For those of you who have used my *Cold Calling Is A Waste Of Time* home study course (NeverColdCall.com), you learned about the concept of filters and amplifiers in marketing. Guess what? Forcing someone to register before he or she buys is a huge filter that's costing you sales! The key to success is a very simple one-page checkout that's short enough for people to complete and click "Order Now" before they change their minds.

- Abandoned shopping cart. This is yet another overlooked strategy that can really explode your sales volume without any increase in traffic. On my sites, for every one person who buys a product, at least ten visit the shopping cart then click the "back" button without ever buying. With abandoned cart features, those people who leave the page without buying will receive a short series of automated e-mails from me, complete with a link that takes them right back to the very shopping cart they abandoned, complete with the correct products, quantity, pricing, and shipping just as they'd originally chosen. This is an extremely powerful and important part of any Internet marketing business funnel.

- Up-sell. After someone buys, but before his or her order is completed, the person is presented with a one-time offer to get a companion or related product for half-off. And believe me, it's a true one-time offer. My server tracks IP addresses, host names, and cookies to make it very difficult for that customer to ever see the offer again. You may think that it's smarter to give him or her a second or third chance to buy the special offer, but that will backfire. Why? Because, remember, building a large list and a loyal following is the single most important thing you can do to succeed online. In building that relationship, your list is going to get to know both you and your marketing tactics. If you continue offering the same special deal over and over, the people on your list will realize that all of your one-time offers are bogus and that they can always get them again in the future. By having a strict one-time offer policy, however, and never allowing anyone to buy after he or she has already seen the offer—unless there is a very good reason—your list will understand that your one-time offers are the real deal. If they miss out on one, guess what will happen the next time they see a one-time offer from you? That's right—they'll buy it, without hesitation. So, while it may seem counterintuitive to deny people who miss a one-time offer and ask for it again in the future, in reality this technique has been responsible for significant growth in my business and sales volume.

- Additional up-sell(s). If someone says yes to an up-sell, chances are he or she will continue saying yes. Many people will buy everything you offer them. I recently added several additional up-sells to my online offers, and they have added thousands of dollars in additional revenue each week, with no increase in traffic. I know someone who has made millions by presenting the customer with a series of five—yes, five—one-time offers after the customer buys the front-end product. As long as the customer continues buying, he or she will continue to see special offers until that person finally stops buying. And what happens when the customer finally say no? That's explained in the next step.

- Down-sell. The down-sell is extremely effective with people who refuse your one-time offer up-sell. Let's say you have a product that sells for $197, and you make a one-time offer for approximately half-price, or $97. A customer who declines to purchase is then presented with an even better offer—perhaps a "lite" version of the $97 product for only $47. This down-sell technique, when done effectively, frequently captures sales from up to half of the people who initially said no. It's another one of those hidden little secrets that you can use to substantially increase your sales volume, without getting a single additional visitor to your site. By the way, you may notice that I keep talking about making more money without generating any additional traffic. Sure, you initially need to generate traffic to get an Internet business off the ground, but getting the most out of your sites is far more important than getting more visitors. Only when you have exhausted testing and implementing of new ideas and have maxed out your site's income potential should you begin spending substantial amounts of time on generating more traffic.
- Thank-you page—viral marketing. Finally, after all of this, the new customer reaches the order thank-you page. On this page I say, "Your order confirmation, support contact, and frequently asked questions are on the lower half of this page," and then present customers with the viral tell-a-friend tool one more time (ViralMaximizer.com). Because most new customers are excited about their purchase, they're not only willing but frequently eager to share the news with their friends. As a result, not only do more people use the tool at this point, but many will send out to their entire address book—frequently thousands of people.
- Thank-you page—membership/social site. Below the viral tell-a-friend tool, I also invite customers to join a free membership site (RecessionCrusher.com) that includes tons of valuable free downloads and social networking features so they

can communicate and chat with other users of my products. Of course, after registering, they're presented with yet another viral invitation tool. (The importance of viral marketing cannot be emphasized too much.)

- Follow-up. A series of automated follow-up e-mails then goes out to new customers indefinitely, or at least until they unsubscribe. Most important, an e-mail goes out shortly after the purchase date reminding them of how the credit card charge will appear on their statement. This prevents people from disputing credit card charges that they don't recognize. These disputes result in costly chargebacks, for which your bank will impose hefty fees and that can even get your processing rates raised, much in the same way that a traffic ticket can cause your car insurance to go up. Beyond that, future offers and new products are announced to customers via that list, as well as free product updates for qualifying products.

- Support. Naturally, your customers will need a way to contact you in the event of problems, cancellation requests, and so on. For that I have a simple support ticket help desk on my server, and the work is outsourced to a small staff who handle customer service issues courteously and promptly. By adding an FAQ section to the help desk page, providing answers to the most commonly asked questions, our ticket volume dropped dramatically (to about one-third of the previous volume), freeing my staff to handle other work. If you are starting out or still have a relatively small business, you can handle the help desk yourself, although I don't recommend doing so because your time can be better spent improving your business, especially when you consider that about 80 percent of support tickets come from problem customers and other troublemakers who are trying to scam you for free products or other concessions.

- Affiliate marketing (after the sale). While there are many ways to monetize your e-mail list beyond selling products and services directly, I'd like to list affiliate marketing here because it's one of the easiest. Due to the size of my e-mail list, it's not uncommon for me to promote someone else's product to my list—only high-quality products that I've reviewed or use myself, of course—and receive a five-figure commission check in the mail a few weeks later. So, keep in mind that as you build a strong business, there will be more and more opportunities for you to multiply your income beyond just selling your own product.

So, there you have it—a simplified explanation of a very effective Internet marketing funnel. Although it may not seem simple right now, don't worry. It will all be explained throughout the course of this book.

With that in mind, let's move on to Part II, and begin covering the hands-on techniques.

Part II

BUILDING A BRAND ONLINE

5

Your Online Identity: The Foundation of Internet Marketing Success

You're probably wondering why we're not jumping right into building a web site and a list.

Slow down. We'll get to that soon enough. However, before you can do that effectively, you need a strong foundation.

A platform.

What is a platform?

A platform, to put it simply, is the overall foundation upon which you will build your Internet empire. That's why I suggest you work on platform building before jumping into trying to sell anything online. Part of the contradiction in that statement is that you will build your platform over time as you sell products, but you still need to keep your future goals in mind all the time in order to build it effectively.

I get questions such as these from budding entrepreneurs and eager Internet marketers all the time.

"How can I make big money as an affiliate?"

"How can I become a best-selling author like you?"

"How can I make millions selling products online?"

"How can I attract hundreds of people to pay to see me speak?"

And so on.

The answer to each of those questions is the same: Build a solid platform. A strong foundation.

Because I have built a solid business platform—and worked to evolve that platform into a brand—I can now do anything online. I can be a best-selling author, over and over. I can launch products off that platform and make big money every time. I can receive substantial speaking fees. I can make a small fortune by consulting (although I don't because I prefer not to work anymore). I can make six figures a year simply promoting other people's products, which takes me a whopping five minutes to send an e-mail out to my list.

I can also expand into other markets and even other totally non-related opportunities via my platform.

A friend of mine became a reality television star because of his strong platform.

Let's take it a step further: With a strong platform and online identity, you can really do anything. Want to become a highly regarded political commentator or blogger? It's easy when you already stand on a strong platform. Maybe you are an aspiring musician or entertainer. Got a strong platform? It's easy to use it to turn your path in life toward any direction you choose. (Few people know that the multimillionaire comedian, Larry the Cable Guy, was a conservative political commentator with a strong platform before turning to comedy.)

I mentioned earlier that no matter what someone asks me regarding Internet marketing success, my first answer always is, "Build a strong platform, then come back to me when you've done that." When someone already has a strong platform, I'm a bit more specific. For example, a well-known entrepreneur approached me recently at a marketing seminar, asking how he could become a

New York Times best-selling author. Knowing that he already had a solid platform, I invited him to my office where, over the course of a few hours, I told him everything I know about getting on the best-seller list.

If he'd asked about making millions selling products online, or as an affiliate—or anything else—I would have gladly told him everything I know.

But only because he already had the platform.

Think of a platform as the wall in a racquetball court. It's solid, and whenever you hit the ball that way, it always comes back. A solid business platform is the same—bounce anything at it and it will always bounce back, be it a book, a product launch, an Internet business, or something different.

However, hit that same racquetball into sand and nothing happens. It stays there. It doesn't bounce back. And that's the fate anyone will face if they attempt to do big things online without first building a solid foundation.

Part of the reason many would-be Internet marketers fail is because they are only looking for end-game and techniques.

What is end-game?

Here's an example: If you want to become a top NASCAR driver but don't know how to drive a car, you first need to learn how to drive. Then you need to become proficient at it. Only then would you even begin the process of learning how to drive a race car—and win.

The problem in the Internet marketing world is that not only are most people looking for fast and easy techniques, but that is what most of the Internet marketing educational products are teaching.

You might make a few thousand dollars a month by only learning techniques, but it's doubtful you will become financially free that way, and you certainly won't become a millionaire. All you will do is create a part-time job for yourself that will never grow into anything more.

Why?

When I started out online, my initial short-term goal was to quit my job. And I did that in about six weeks, because in that time the income from my online business was equal to the income from my job, which, without bragging, was quite high itself (I was the top salesman in our company region, selling very large and expensive business and call-center telephone systems).

Initially I had goals of making a million dollars, or $10 million, or $20 thousand a month. (Interestingly, that last one did the most for me during my learning process, when I realized that consistent recurring income is more important than a big one-time hit. More on that later.)

But it wasn't until I settled on the modest goal of quitting my job—making only $3,000 per month, enough to pay my bills without struggling—did things really begin to happen for me.

As I said, within six weeks, I was free from my job and making $6,000 dollars per month to boot—double my initial goal!

It only took me a few weeks to get there. I only waited so long to quit my job because I couldn't yet believe my eyes and was afraid the income stream would suddenly dry up.

It didn't.

Quite the contrary, in fact. And that's why I reduced my goal to the humble amount of $3,000 a month, enough to quit my job. I learned that gem of wisdom from Robert Kiyosaki, who said, "I quit my job so I could get rich!" You see, if you're trying to build a business on the side while maintaining a day job, you'll never have enough time to devote to that business to make you wealthy. It will stagnate and you'll have just enough time to keep it running.

Without a job, however, you can devote all of your time to your business. That's when the big killing will come.

Only seven months later I was writing a check for my dream car, a Mercedes-Benz S500, something that seemed completely out of reach only a short time prior.

Barely three years later, I was moving to my dream locale, a town which many authorities, including *Forbes*, have named the most expensive in America.

In between my book became a *New York Times* bestseller and even held the #1 spot on Amazon during the same week that Ann Coulter launched one of her books with seemingly 24/7 cable news coverage and a huge promotional effort.

I don't state any of this to brag. I do so to illustrate the difference between building a business on a solid platform and achieving your dream lifestyle, versus trying to get rich quick with techniques and barely making a few thousand a month, breaking even, or, worse, going broke.

I know several marketers who started before me who now make upwards of $10 million dollars per year.

Which will you choose?

In the following four chapters, I'll explain a variety of steps you can take to build a bulletproof platform and enter the world of Internet marketing on a very strong foundation!

6

CREATE INSTANT (AND VERIFIABLE) EXPERT STATUS

Ahh, the written word.

People believe what they see in print. This is a proven fact; it applies to everyone from biased media outlets to expert marketers to the old television show *Candid Camera*.

On a 1963 episode of *Candid Camera*, the crew covered up a "Welcome to Delaware" sign on Interstate 95 with a sign reading, "Delaware is Closed" while leaving the highway wide open and not blocked in any way.

Cars came screeching to a halt.

People begged and pleaded with the fake security guard, crying, "I need to get in there! My family is in there!" The guards simply replied with, "Sorry, Delaware is under repair and we don't have specifics. Try again tomorrow."

Sure, it sounds ridiculous, but it's true. This really happened!

That's the power of the written word.

Now, let's be fair here: People won't believe the written word all of the time. It depends on context—how that written word is presented and by whom. The *Candid Camera* stunt worked because it appeared to be official, complete with fake officials manning the sign. Dubious media outlets get away with it because most people assume the media to be official and therefore telling the truth. (Of course, this isn't always the case—remember Dan Rather's firing from CBS several years ago for knowingly broadcasting a made-up story.)

With that in mind, what is one of the most credibility-lending terms in the world of the written word?

That's right: Author.

Even better: Expert Author.

If you want to have credibility to such an extent that people believe what you say and trust you to the point of buying from you without any doubts or fears, you really need to get that title of Expert Author beneath your name.

This is something I did early on and it contributed greatly not only to the success of my business, but also to my becoming a published author and subsequently a *New York Times* best-selling author.

Disclaimer: I need to point out the value of honesty and integrity. Expert Author status will only work as long as you have a positive reputation. You need to sell quality products or services and back them. You can't sell garbage and you can't rip people off. You can't provide poor customer service and expect to get away with it, especially now with thousands of review and complaint sites all over the Internet.

With that out of the way, here's how it works: There are thousands of free reprint articles web sites all over the Internet. These sites allow you to upload well-written articles where they are not only available to read, but where other web site owners, bloggers, and newsletter and magazine publishers can download and reprint them for free, with the one condition that they must also print your full bio including any web site links you provide.

This has multiple effects: It provides valuable links to your web site, which will bring it up high in search engine rankings. It generates valuable leads for you, as the result of people who read your article (and it had better be good) and subsequently visit your web site or call you to buy. It has a viral effect as more people read your article and then reprint it on their own sites or in their newsletters.

But the icing on the cake is this: The top free reprint article web site and one that I use personally, EzineArticles.com, ranks extremely highly in search engines.

Go to Google right now, type in my name, Frank Rumbauskas, and what do you see in the top half of rankings?

That's right: Frank Rumbauskas—EzineArticles.com Expert Author.

As long as you provide quality content—meaning unbiased, useful information, without any selling or self-promotion—EzineArticles.com will accept your articles and list you as an Expert Author.

There are many hefty benefits to this. First of all, anyone who looks you up online is going to see that Expert Author result. Because of EzineArticles.com's page rank with Google, it will always appear very high in search results, so they'll see it right away. This is doubly important in a world where high-ranking complaint sites are all over the Internet and society's entitlement mentality is growing, resulting in bogus complaints and Better Business Bureau reports from problem customers who will file a report the moment you don't give them everything they demand for free.

In short, this one technique gets your name all over the Internet, even more so if you submit to multiple article directories. There are even low-cost services that automatically upload your article to thousands of sites, resulting in thousands of search results when someone googles your name—that's prominence!

It gets you plenty of traffic, and I even know people who have done nothing other than article marketing to generate a substantial flow of traffic and significant income.

Now, let's look at the other side of Expert Author status.

When I became a *New York Times* best-selling author, I immediately inserted those words beneath my name and photo on all of my sites. Sales instantly increased significantly.

Even though you may not be a *New York Times* bestseller today (although you can if you choose to and work to build a solid business foundation), you can add those words, Expert Author, to your name and photo on your site.

This is instant and verifiable credibility, since anyone who decides to run a Google search to verify will see that right before their eyes in search listings.

Use Expert Author everywhere. web sites, blogs, Twitter, on your business cards, you name it. This technique is free and easy—all you have to do is take the time to write one or more high-quality articles about your industry or the market you serve, and upload them. Look me up on EzineArticles.com for examples.

This is the first, easiest, and most basic step to building a strong platform, so get to it right now—don't hesitate!

7

GENERATE INSTANT (AND VERIFIABLE) ONLINE MEDIA COVERAGE

Now that you're on your way after creating your Expert Author status (you did it before moving on, didn't you?), let's get your name in the news.

Think about it: What could give you more credibility than being quoted in mainstream media outlets as an expert in your field?

To tell you the truth, not much (as long as you're not referred to in the story as "the defendant"). The results from this one are up there with *New York Times* best-seller status.

The secret lies in strategic use of press releases, another tool that most people consider out of reach and accessible only to major corporations, but now it has become available to anyone thanks to the Internet.

Have you ever used Yahoo! News? I do—I refer to Yahoo! frequently to check on weather, latest general-interest news, and more. As a result, I'm very familiar with the look and feel of a Yahoo! News story, as are most Internet users (read: tens of millions of people).

If you're aspiring to make it big online, you've undoubtedly been frustrated by seeing phrases like "Best-Selling Author" under people's names (I've already taught you how to get around that one), or media credentials. On many marketers' sites, you'll see a list of the major outlets in which they've been quoted, interviewed, or featured. You may think it's going to take years of work and that you'll have to succeed first in order to get media attention later, but you couldn't be more wrong.

In reality, I became successful online because of my success in getting myself in the news. In other words, getting myself into the news came first, when I was still a nobody, and my major successes springboarded from that. Never forget the racquetball metaphor for a solid platform.

Specifically, if you are starting with nothing—no foundation—you can quickly, easily, and inexpensively get yourself quoted as a top expert in your field in online news outlets such as Yahoo! News, Google News, and many more.

Here's how the process works: First, write a newsworthy story that quotes you as an expert. Here's an example of a release I used that was very effective for me:

Sales Results Show that Cold Calling is Dead
Sales results and studies show that cold calling doesn't work anymore. Frank Rumbauskas learned this the hard way when he entered the sales profession fourteen years ago. Creator of NeverColdCall .com, he has now taught over ten thousand salespeople how to sell without cold calling.

Phoenix, AZ (PRWEB) January 10, 2006. For years, cold calling has been the method of choice for finding new customers for salespeople everywhere. "However, today's economy has made cold calling obsolete," says Frank Rumbauskas, the foremost authority on the death of cold calling.

"Twenty years ago you could cold call and sell something. Nowadays, that simply annoys people and is frequently illegal. Cold calling

is dead, and new and innovative ways to attract prospects are in," he said.

Since starting www.nevercoldcall.com almost three years ago, over ten thousand salespeople have implemented his Cold Calling Is a Waste of Time *sales system and are successfully selling more without any cold calling whatsoever. As he points out, however, the shift away from cold calling is difficult for many to accept.*

"In most companies, cold calling is the sole method of generating business. Managers and trainers simply haven't accepted the reality that cold calling doesn't work in today's complex world," says Rumbauskas.

He also warns that many employers have an ulterior motive in mandating cold calling.

"Cold calling is a way for companies to avoid marketing costs. They have the sales force cold call instead, which of course is done at the salesperson's expense. It's a tremendous waste of time and money for salespeople and ultimately leads to failure, but it's an easy way for companies to cut short-term costs," he said.

Rumbauskas cites numerous reasons for the death of cold calling, including a comprehensive study done by the Kenan-Flagler Business School at the University of North Carolina, which concluded that over 80 percent of executives absolutely will not accept cold calls. He points out that dozens of ways now exist to prospect without cold calling, so you have everything to lose and nothing to gain by offending prospects with cold calls.

For more information, or to obtain Frank Rumbauskas' free e-book, Cold Calling, *please visit* www.nevercoldcall.com.

As you can see, I wrote the story referring to myself in the third person. You need to make it sound like it's coming from a journalist and not from yourself—this is very important. Also, it must be factual. You can't make any false claims or you'll get a call from the release service explaining that they can't send out your release until you verify all claims made in it.

Next, go to PRWeb.com and create an account. Once that's all set up, you'll want to choose their basic option ($80 at the time of this writing) and submit your release. Follow their guidelines carefully to guarantee quick acceptance.

Once you get a confirmation e-mail that your release has been accepted and is queued to send, you're done.

In just a day or two it will go out, and your release will appear as a very real news story in Yahoo! News, Google News, Topix, and other news outlets.

Once your release is distributed, I suggest that you immediately look up the article in various news outlets and save them (print to .pdf is suggested as you can simply send out the .pdf file or display it on your web site).

On your home page and "About" page, add the logos of all the media outlets where your story appeared.

Send a link to the story out to your list. I love doing this with Yahoo! News because of the easy "e-mail to a friend" link in all their articles, causing it to go viral. The increased views will cause it to rank higher in both Yahoo! News as well as PRWeb.com, giving you more and more visibility.

Okay, that's how you get instant credibility for yourself. But what if you really want to get serious exposure in the news, above and beyond generating instant credibility?

Paul Hartunian (EasyNewsCoverage.com), the leading expert on getting press coverage, explains a simple three-step process to test, track, and exploit press releases for maximum potential.

First, submit your release to a free press release site (just google the term "free press releases"). All press release services include statistics, including the number of media outlets who have picked up your release. That's the number we're concerned with here, not total views.

After your release is distributed by a free service, take a look at the stats. If it has been picked up by at least a few media outlets, it's time to move on to step two.

This time, go to WebWire.com and go for their basic offering ($20 at the time of this writing). Submit your release there, and, again, check stats. If there are a respectable number of media outlet pickups, go to PRWeb.com and release it via their basic offering (Paul Hartunian explains that PRWeb's basic level, $80 at the time of this writing, will give you everything you need and that the higher-priced options are not necessary.)

The purpose here is to verify that your release will actually get picked up by media outlets without spending $80 every time. (Naturally, this is irrelevant if you merely want to get your name in the press for the reasons described earlier in this chapter.)

If your release is getting some respectable hits, and you really want to take things to the next level, get online and search for "fax broadcast press release services." These services aren't free—you'll have to pay depending on volume—but they can immediately fax your press release to the release lines at literally tens of thousands of media outlets. Just be sure to do it with a high-quality release that has proven itself at the PRWeb.com $80 level.

One final thought: If you're going to follow the former strategy to generate instant news stories—and you should if it's your first release—then you should include a hyperlink to your web site in it. The reason is to provide powerful backlinks to your site, which will be picked up by search engines and will increase your search rankings. However, if you're using the latter strategy to get widespread news coverage, then avoid including backlinks, because releases that include them rarely get picked up by media outlets. There you have it—instant credibility and exposure in real media outlets.

Don't underestimate this. If you're looking to buy a product and only one of the providers you look at has media credentials, doesn't that provider suddenly look a lot better than the others?

Get started now on your first press release, and remember to save copies of the story, especially in major outlets like Yahoo! News and Topix. It's another very important building block in establishing your platform, so do it *now*!

8

POSITION YOURSELF FOR ONGOING MEDIA COVERAGE AND CREDIBILITY

The beautiful thing about getting some media coverage for yourself is that once you get the ball rolling, it becomes easier and easier to get press. It's sort of like what wealthy self-made people say all the time: "The first million is the hardest. After that, it's easy."

The same is true with media. What most people don't realize is how competitive media outlets are—if they see a competitor running a story that they haven't run yet, they're on it fast! That's why every time you see a television news program or newspaper breaking a new story, every other station and paper jumps right on the bandwagon.

In this chapter, I'm going to show you how to leverage your self-made media coverage to get more and more with a wide range of media types.

If you've executed the steps in the previous three chapters—and perhaps gotten some bites from a press release—then you will have more than enough to build an ongoing media platform that will keep your name consistently in the news. No, you're not going to appear on major television news programs—although you can if you really put the time and effort into it—but you can and will get yourself into major business magazines, practically endless trade and industry journals, newspapers and radio, and even on local television news programs.

What's the point, you might say?

I've already explained the importance of being able to show media credentials in your marketing collateral, your web site(s), even your business cards. Doing those things will get you more business and dramatically increase your sales, but becoming a media figure holds far more potential than that.

Take a look at my business: One of my income streams is public speaking (paid speaking, where I'm paid up-front just to appear, not platform selling where I may or may not get paid depending on who the audience is).

I'm not going to explain the benefits of public speaking (even free speaking) here. However, I will tell you that the speaking business, particularly in the sales niche, is unbelievably competitive. For every high-fee speaker like me (nearly all are fellow best-selling authors), there are hundreds willing to speak for little or no money in order to promote themselves and their books.

In a business that competitive, it takes an extra edge to win gigs.

One of the most powerful weapons I have at my disposal is my media coverage. By sending the prospective client articles from major magazines like *Entrepreneur* and *Selling Power*, copies of newspaper clippings, lists of radio interviews, the rare television appearance, my Expert Author articles, countless articles on various blogs and web sites, including the ones I taught you how to create in Chapter 7—I have an instant, verifiable level of expertise, credibility, and most important, *value*, when compared with my competitors.

Just for the record, I do not get speaking gigs as a result of my best-selling author status. Quite the contrary. After I became a bestseller, I expected the phone to start ringing and the speaking requests to come pouring in.

Not so.

Baffled, I scheduled a consultation with Vickie Sullivan, one of the leading experts in the world of paid speaking, who explained to me that I was not getting any requests *because* I was a best-selling author! Potential clients assume that any major best-selling author will be too expensive, and they won't even bother calling.

As you can see, some of the advantages that people assume I have frequently work against me. In your case, however, you can use media credentials to break into the profitable world of paid speaking, since even most best-selling authors don't know the techniques in this book and fail to get any real coverage despite being a bestseller.

On the topic of authors, by the way, that's another profitable world you can break into with media credentials. Although they do have publicists, most publishers typically seek out authors who already have prominence and visibility, since it greatly reduces their risk of a failed book.

Those are two examples of what ongoing media coverage can do for you. Now let's move on to the actual techniques.

First of all, you should now have:

- Your Expert Author articles.
- Your "placed" Yahoo! News, Google News, and other press release articles.
- Actual news stories as a result of your press release(s) being picked up by outlets.

The first thing you'll need to do is to assemble copies of all of the above (within reason—if you've written dozens of articles, just pick the one or two best) and assemble them into what's known as a media kit.

Your media kit will be your brochure of sorts for getting more and more media coverage. And if you're a salesperson or small business owner, you'll certainly want to include the kit with any sales collateral and proposals. Use a simple presentation folder with your articles on one side and your news stories on the other. Include one or two business cards.

You'll also want to save all of the above as .pdf files and compress them into a zip archive for easy posting on your web site, as well as easily e-mailing them to prospective clients.

If you're strictly an Internet marketer and don't do any direct selling, you'll absolutely need to post the media kit on your site— your main or hub site as well as blogs and various marketing sites.

Once that's done, the next step is to compile a list of all your local media outlets. Prepare a media kit for each one, include a professional and polite cover letter briefly stating that you are a local resident and/or business owner, that you are including previous media coverage and articles you've written, and invite them to contact you should they want to do an article, interview, or even a small blurb in their publication or show.

You'll be surprised at the response. Local media outlets frequently have trouble finding enough interesting people and stories to fill their space every day, and many will be eager to chat with you.

After you get some hits with this strategy, you can do another mailing to other local outlets—the ones who didn't call—and send a copy of the article or story that a competitor has run. This will really pique their interest, due to the competitive nature of media.

With a nice portfolio of local media under your belt, it's time to kick things up a notch and start going for state and national media. Again, mail out media kits. Make sure you're hitting them with your press release fax broadcasts, if you're using that service. Don't forget relevant magazines.

Many people I know who you've never heard of have gotten national press coverage this way.

Now that I've explained all the proactive ways to get press, it's time for the other one, and it happens to be my personal favorite.

ProfNet (NewsQueryWire.com) is a service costing $97/month at the time of this writing, but worth many times that in terms of media access, coverage, and the profits that will result from its service.

ProfNet is used by journalists who are in need of information, quotes, or interview subjects for stories. They post queries to the network, explaining something like the following (relevant to my niche): "I'm seeking sales experts, authors, and executives to comment on a story I'm writing for the *New York Times* about what salespeople can do to have a competitive edge in the current economic recession."

As a well-known authority on sales, I'd respond with something like, "Hi, my name is Frank Rumbauskas. I'm the author of the *New York Times* bestseller *Never Cold Call Again* and I've also been featured or interviewed in *Selling Power, Entrepreneur, Investor's Business Daily*, and many more. Here's my take on how salespeople can do well in a recession . . ." And then I'd list two or three bullet points, concise sentences, or tips that salespeople can use to excel in a recession. Notice how I mentioned my previous coverage right up front—that's why it's so important to get some coverage in order to maximize the value of this technique.

These queries come in all the time, too numerous to get to them all, and for every industry and niche you can imagine.

One of my favorite things about the ProfNet service is that you not only get press in major, otherwise inaccessible publications, but also numerous radio interviews as well as the rare television appearance.

But the one thing I really love is that you will, over time, get to know and build relationships with real heavy-hitter free-lance writers, the ones who write for huge circulation magazines and newspapers. Treat them well, be polite, always give valuable information, and they'll remember you. The next time they are on deadline for a story related to your niche, they'll skip the query process and simply e-mail you direct.

That's powerful. And your competition won't stand a chance.

Particularly if you're a small business owner in a competitive industry, the media credentials you'll be able to display and call your own will completely blow away your competition, especially if you contact local media regularly. All it takes is a few mentions of your name, and while people may not remember you exactly, they'll know they've heard of you and that's all it takes to win a sale against an unknown competitor.

9

OFFLINE IDENTITY BUILDERS TO BOOST YOUR ONLINE RESULTS

There are obviously lots of ways to bring yourself tremendous credibility online, as you've now seen.

You can give yourself Expert Author status—and get massive visibility and web traffic—by writing informative articles and uploading them to the proper directories.

You can create news stories about yourself, giving you immediate media exposure and again bringing you web traffic and prospective new customers.

You can get your stories picked up by multiple media outlets by gradually increasing the level of press release service and only releasing the most effective ones through the highest-cost services.

You can even get reporters to call you, and build relationships over time to get consistent and repeated coverage in serious print and media outlets.

Having said all that, there are still things you can do in the good old-fashioned offline world—as well as online—that will exponentially multiply the effects of all this coverage, multiply your sales by huge margins, and give you a level of credibility beyond your wildest dreams.

While most people who want to learn how to market online will only look for online techniques by default, old-fashioned credentials are what we're talking about here: certifications, continuing education, past accomplishments, and other gems that you can include in your bio, mention in your articles and news releases, and of course, display prominently on your web site(s).

For example, I sell an educational product online that teaches Internet marketers how to use Google AdWords, from the very basics through advanced techniques (AdWordsInsideSecrets .com). After creating the product, test-marketing it to make sure it would sell, getting testimonials from a small group of people to whom I sent prerelease copies, and of course getting the web site built and creating the marketing systems, I did one more thing before going live.

Google offers a certification program for AdWords, allowing individuals who pass a comprehensive test and who have successfully used AdWords for the minimum time required to be certified. The certification includes an impressive logo that all certified individuals can display anywhere, including web sites, business cards, or anywhere else, and because I already knew all there was to know about AdWords, having used it successfully for over six years, I signed up, passed the test very quickly and easily, and was able to immediately begin calling myself a Google-Certified AdWords Professional, and most important, to display that logo on the product web site.

I didn't even bother split-testing the results of having that seal on my web site versus not having it. The test would be pointless and would cost me sales because I already know that such a certification greatly increases sales.

What certifications can you get that are relevant to your product or service?

What have you accomplished in your past that seems totally irrelevant but that would boost your sales?

Here's a good example: A friend of mine who markets online is a former Marine. After completing basic training at Parris Island—years and years ago when he was 18 years old—he graduated from boot camp as the #1 Honor Graduate.

While it may seem like it happened too long ago and is irrelevant to his current Internet marketing businesses, it works. It's a big deal. Graduating #1 Honor Graduate from Marine Corps boot camp is the equivalent of graduating from high school or college as the valedictorian. It may seem even more impressive to people who are familiar with the extreme level of difficulty of Marine boot camp—especially other Marines!

Another thing to consider is educational status. For example, I recently purchased a software product costing nearly $1,000. One of the factors that persuaded me to buy it over less expensive alternatives was the fact that the author of the software is a PhD and always displays that title after his name.

When I'm considering an advanced piece of software that was created by an individual—not a large corporation like Apple or Microsoft—and that could potentially wreak havoc on my business if it doesn't perform as advertised, knowing that it was written by a PhD is important to me, even if the degree isn't directly related to the product.

I assume that the guy is smart, and that's all I care about.

If you're an up-and-coming marketer, author, or expert in your field, and you would like to break into paid speaking, the National Speakers Association (NSA) would be a good place to start. NSA membership isn't open to everyone—you have to verify that you've done a minimum amount of speaking—and people know that. It's a way for someone to verify that you're an experienced speaker without having to call a list of references or previous clients.

When I co-authored an insurance sales training program with a top-producing life insurance agent, I realized that my credibility might be on the line if I wasn't also a licensed agent. Therefore, I bought a home-study course, learned everything I had to know to pass the test, and obtained my insurance agent license. I took that a step further by getting my business licensed as a broker (for those unfamiliar with the insurance business, agents work for brokers, who are in turn contracted with the actual insurance providers).

When I'm marketing products to salespeople, I constantly remind them that I was a top producing sales representative, routinely breaking company records, winning trips and awards, and even boasting an 80 percent close rate, all without cold calling.

When I'm marketing to Internet marketers, I tell the story of how I quit my last job and retired from active work less than six weeks after starting my business, and only waited that long because I couldn't believe it was true—and then wrote a check for my dream S-Class Mercedes-Benz only six months after that.

When I'm marketing to Google AdWords advertisers, I remind them that I'm a Google-Certified AdWords Professional, and that I used Google AdWords not only to explode my business but also to become a *New York Times* best-selling author.

What have you done in your past, or what certification, licenses, and so on do you have, that you can tell prospective customers and display on your web site and marketing materials?

The possibilities are endless!

Taking this idea a step further, getting outside certification for your business massively improves trust.

Have you ever seen the Better Business Bureau logo on business materials, or seen the BBB Online seal on web sites? They exist to generate trust, and let customers know that you're an honest business that delivers as promised and doesn't rip people off.

On my web sites, I use the GuaranteeGuarantee seal (GuaranteeGuarantee.com), an independent watchdog group that monitors online merchants and verifies that they honor their money-back guarantees 100 percent of the time, no questions asked.

Numerous security-verification seals are commonly seen on web sites like VeriSign's, letting prospective customers know that your servers and security measures meet the necessary requirements to protect their credit card number and other private information.

Do this right now: Put this book down, take out a notebook and pen, and begin brainstorming all the things you can use to boost your credibility, online and off. Then, once that's done, get them on your web site! Put the most impressive ones—things like my Google certification—on your home page where people will see them immediately. Sprinkle less relevant ones throughout your web site, and include them in the "About" page.

Little steps like this are like big, heavy bricks in the solid business foundation that you're building.

Part III

BUILDING BUZZ ONLINE

10

WHAT IS BUZZ?

Do you know what buzz is? Buzz, quite simply, is getting people talking about you. Creating word-of-mouth. Generating excitement and curiosity to make people want to get involved.

As I write this, my friend Mike Filsaime is about to launch a new product—a new release of his Butterfly Marketing system (BMManuscript.com).

However, Mike isn't just releasing the product and mailing it out to his list, along with his affiliates' lists.

No.

You see, to make really big money online, you need to create buzz.

Mike first got all of his affiliates on board and made sure they had active affiliate accounts and were fully aware of the new product and its subsequent launch.

Then, he began sprinkling his list and those of his affiliates with sneaky teaser e-mails, letting them know something big is coming soon, but not revealing the whole story.

Next, Mike put together several case studies, true and verifiable stories of people who had used the original first edition of Butterfly Marketing to make millions of dollars in income. He then had his video production people create videos showcasing those case studies.

After that, e-mails began going out to Mike's list and the affiliates' lists, telling people to go to a web site where they could view the case studies and simultaneously get an instant download of the previous version of the product, for free! The case studies were periodically changed every few days and replaced with new ones, and the requisite e-mails would then go out to all lists letting people know and reminding them that they could get the free download as well.

Oh yeah, one more thing: Every e-mail and every web page reminded people that while thousands of people are visiting the site and signing up for advance notification of the actual product release date and time, only 5,000 copies have been printed and will be available.

All of this built up a tremendous amount of anticipation, and most importantly, buzz.

People were excitedly e-mailing each other, talking about it, and discussing it in blogs and online forums.

As a result, a huge amount of word-of-mouth spread all over the world. This brought more and more people into the fold, and they watched the videos, read the e-mails, got the free download, and got excited. They started talking about it, and on and on.

I know how effective this technique is: I'm friends with the owner of Mike's web hosting company, who has himself and his staff on high alert every time Mike does one of these buzz-worthy launches out of fear that Mike's traffic will crash the entire data center—because it happened the first time!

The beauty of launches like these is that not only does the product sell out almost immediately—that's the power of scarcity—but it will continue to sell like mad even after the promotional period expires or the product is rereleased to the general public.

Why? Because, with all the excitement generated up-front, the buzz continues for months and years. People will keep buying after the launch ends, even if they must pay a higher price or forfeit bonuses or miss out on other goodies.

That's the power of buzz.

Look at Apple's iPhone. They did a similar excitement-building, high energy pre-launch campaign just like Mike's. Since I didn't yet own an iPhone, I decided to get one when the 3G version finally came out. There was a problem, however: I couldn't get one until a month later.

Every time I attempted to buy one, one of two things happened: Either every local Apple store was completely sold out, or they had them in stock but there was a two-hour line. And there are three Apple stores within 15 minutes of my home and office.

I used a powerful buzz-building launch process on my best-selling book, *Never Cold Call Again* (John Wiley & Sons, 2006) that, along with other strategies included in this book, catapulted it to #1 on Amazon.com within hours and also sent it to the *New York Times* best-seller list.

For several weeks prior to the announcement, I peppered my list with videos, case studies, and other teasers that would bring up different challenges salespeople face, and their solutions. As I got closer to the launch date, the message changed from "This is a common problem, and here's the solution," to "This is a common problem, and next Tuesday you'll get the answer."

Next Tuesday, of course, was the book's launch date.

The Friday and Monday just before launch day, subscribers received two final e-mails telling them to set their alarms for 10:00 AM Eastern time on Tuesday, because not only would they finally get the answers they'd been searching for, but there would also be lots of extra goodies that they'd miss out on if they didn't act immediately.

Not surprisingly, the book did exceptionally well. In fact, very recently, a different publisher who was trying to convince me to sign with them said, "Since it came out three years ago, *Never Cold Call Again* has been the sales book to beat."

Yes, I know it's a great book because of all the great reviews and the endless success stories I hear from readers, but it wasn't the book's quality that made it "the sales book to beat." It's all about the buzz. In fact, the overwhelming majority of published books fail, and, contrary to popular belief, only a tiny fraction of published authors are wealthy.

As I tell people, I spend two weeks every year writing a new book and the other 50 weeks selling it. Successful authors are certainly not hermits who write all the time, as movies and television portray them. No—successful authors are effective *marketers* who know how to create buzz. (In case you're wondering, I'm able to write my books so quickly because all of the knowledge is already in my head. I'm simply putting it on paper.)

Another fantastic book that became a huge bestseller through buzz, and even made it onto every single best-seller list in the United States for a while, is *The 4-Hour Work Week* by Timothy Ferriss (Crown, 2007).

Tim has pretty much become famous among other authors as the mastermind on buzz for books.

What Tim did, prior to the book's release date, was send out prerelease copies to hundreds of blog owners all over the world. This resulted in hundreds of blogs posting reviews, talking about how great the book is, and so on. This created enough buzz for the book that by the time it finally hit the bookstores, a feeding frenzy was on to buy it, and it instantly hit the best-seller lists.

Shortly after that, Tim contacted me through a mutual friend, asking for advice on how to sell more books.

My reply?

"Tim, you have it backwards. I want to learn from *you*!"

The funny part of all this is that Tim didn't even use the usual book launch techniques so common today, such as offering a gazillion free downloads to people who bought the book and could prove it with an Amazon.com receipt or order number. He didn't need that, because the buzz he created with his blog owner strategy was all he needed.

After the book hit the best-seller lists, it went on autopilot. It became a big news story, it received tons of media coverage, it was prominently displayed in bookstores and on bookseller web sites, and now, over a year later, it's still a top seller.

Through the rest of Part III of this book, we'll explore various ways to create buzz for yourself and your business.

11

YOUR ONLINE PERSONA WILL MAKE OR BREAK YOU

Before jumping into buzz-building techniques, you'll first need to decide who you want to be online.

This doesn't mean being dishonest about who you are—not at all—but rather, creating an online persona that is true and accurate but is also relevant to your business, your products, and your services.

As you now know, I have several products you probably didn't know about previously, each requiring me to portray a different persona.

When I'm selling to salespeople and sales managers, I'm a sales expert with a proven track record. However, after creating my sales products, I became an Internet marketer. Once the writing and recording were completed, it was my job to market the finished products.

Even though I was through with sales when I quit my last job back in early 2003, and was a full-time Internet marketer from that point forward, I still had to be a sales guy online. In my sales newsletters, I'm a sales expert. In my sales books and products,

I'm a sales expert. At sales-related speaking events, I'm a sales expert.

I couldn't talk about Internet marketing, even though that's what was usually on my mind—it was my new job. However, it would've been the wrong persona to portray while selling sales products. People would've asked, "What can we possibly learn about face-to-face sales from an Internet guy?"

After a few years of generating millions of dollars with my NeverColdCall.com business, I realized I now had another, even more lucrative asset: the knowledge and expertise I'd gained on the subject of Internet marketing.

Even though NeverColdCall.com sells sales products, it is actually powered by Internet marketing knowledge.

At first, I didn't know just how much of a gold mine I'd been sitting on. I first spoke at an Internet marketing seminar on the topic of Google AdWords, but as it turned out, the audience members wanted to know *everything* about Internet marketing. They knew about my success and wanted to learn how to replicate it.

As a result, I continue to write new sales books and occasionally create new sales products, but my current focus is in the Internet marketing world. (This book, of course, straddles both, because it's applicable to salespeople as well as to small business owners and other Internet marketers.)

A very successful dating expert recently followed a similar path. Having made millions of dollars selling dating advice products to men online, he turned to Internet marketing because many others were willing to pay big bucks to learn how he did it. Like me, although his products were about how single men can meet women, his full-time job was Internet marketing. He separates the two personas to an extreme degree, using his real name as the author of his Internet marketing products but using a pen name for the dating products. After all, single men who want to learn how to meet women might assume that an Internet marketer is some kind of computer geek who knows nothing about women, and vice versa. It's good business sense to create a persona that is relevant to the business in question.

When I promote my Google AdWords products, I'm a Google-Certified AdWords professional. When I'm marketing insurance sales products, I'm a licensed insurance agent and partner in a real insurance agency.

You get the point.

If you've read my previous books, you know that a salesperson must be very careful about the job titles used on letterhead and other promotional materials. Account executive, sales representative, account manager, and so on, are all job titles that create the wrong persona. Nobody really wants to meet with a salesperson, so you have to portray yourself differently.

Part II of this book, on building a brand and generating media and other news coverage, had the goal of making you a credible expert in your respective industry. This takes the focus off your sales job title, and transforms you into that expert, someone who is so credible that the prospect would likely pay you for your time as a consultant, let alone buy from you.

Although my most well-known title is that of author, I pull the focus away from that and replace it with sales expert, Internet marketing expert, AdWords expert, and so on, depending on the situation and what I'm marketing.

If I were to start a business related to amateur radio, as another example, I'd note that I obtained the very difficult top license class at the age of fourteen, and would probably obtain additional credentials, such as a commercial radiotelephone license, in the future.

It's your job to do the same. If your day job is accountant, for example, and you're building an online business selling nutritional supplements, again as an example, you certainly won't want to tell prospective customers you're an accountant. You'll want to become a certified personal trainer, get some kind of nutritionist certification, and, of course, exploit various media strategies to get yourself quoted in various media as an expert in the world of nutrition and fitness.

That will do more for your online business than just about anything else.

Then, and only then, would you mention in your bio that you were previously an accountant.

It's time to brainstorm again: Sit down and find out what you can do to create your persona and how you'll convey that persona online, truthfully and accurately, whether you're a salesperson or an Internet marketer.

12

BLOGGING TO CREATE BUZZ

Blogging is huge.

Everyone who is anyone has a blog these days. Translation: If you don't have one—and update it regularly—you're going to be left behind, if you haven't been already.

A blog is an extraordinarily powerful medium. It costs next to nothing to have, yet blogs are moving and shaking the very foundations of just about everything we know about business and media.

Look at how much blogs have changed the world of political news reporting. For decades, a small number of major news networks and a few large newswire services were it. That's where everyone got their news, and as a result, the media had a responsibility to remain at least somewhat objective and report the facts. Sure, there is usually some degree of bias no matter what—every level of compiling and reporting news involves human personalities and opinions—but commentators were still a lot more objective than they are today.

Enter the so-called New Media, which blogs dominate.

Blogs suddenly gave people the ability to become reporters on their own. The Internet is vast and unlimited, and it was easy to put up a blog and start writing your opinions, and political blogs began popping up all over the place.

In particular, people who felt that the mainstream media were becoming biased and unfair began blogging in earnest, presenting the opposing opinion, of course.

The mainstream media, seeing this phenomenon take place, felt obligated to move their views in the opposite direction of the bloggers, seeing this as their way of balancing the playing field.

In response, bloggers who believe that the media must present the news with no bias whatsoever became furious and multiplied their efforts. More blogs were created with their authors writing more and more.

The mainstream media, in response, moved even further in their direction as the bloggers, in turn, continued in their direction.

This endless cycle continues and has created a situation where the media have moved so far off-center that they lost sight of their real job—reporting the facts—and fatally discredited themselves in the 2008 U.S. presidential election.

That lost credibility, in turn, is being transferred to the New Media, which include blogs as well as satellite talk radio and a few other outlets.

Why does this matter to you? Because this newfound credibility gives bloggers far more power than ever before, which you're going to take advantage of.

You already know that people believe what they see in writing. That hasn't always been the case with the Internet, and to a large degree, it still isn't. That's why you need to get yourself in writing before you can expect people to believe what you put on a web site.

Blogs, however, are increasingly achieving the status of news outlets. This creates the effect of people seeing them as writing, and—you guessed it—people believe what you say in writing.

Having a blog has many other benefits. It's a way for you to provide unbiased, useful, informative information to the world, attracting new customers to you. It allows you to build a loyal following. You'll even have fans who add your blogs to their Internet news feeds, anticipating your next post all the time.

Someone I know created a blog during the recent real estate bubble and subsequent crash—posting opinions that defied those of the mainstream media and common beliefs at that time—that grew so large, major book deals were offered to him by publishers. This strategy was based around using controversy to build a large audience, who were so passionate about their opinions that they routinely sent new blog posts to friends and associates, growing the audience virally and therefore very quickly.

Others use blogs to keep their customer bases informed, allowing happy and loyal customers to express their thoughts and questions via comments, and to again forward and share posts to spread the word for the blogger.

Affiliate marketers use blogs to post product reviews that include an affiliate link, giving them a way to earn lucrative commissions without overtly selling.

What can a blog do for you?

If you're a salesperson or small business owner, you need a blog to build and establish your online persona. If you want to be viewed as an expert in *any* area, your blog will go far to take you there.

The gentleman who was offered book deals thanks to his real estate blog isn't a real estate expert by any stretch. He's never worked in real estate, is not a licensed agent, and has no credentials to suggest that he's any kind of real estate expert.

His blog, however, solidified his online persona to such a degree that the book deals came rolling in. Imagine it: An ordinary citizen was being offered big bucks to write a major book on real estate!

It's fine, and sometimes even necessary, to have multiple blogs. I have a sales and marketing blog, wrapped up into one. I have an AdWords blog. I have a political blog to share my views. I even have a satire blog that I used as a publicity stunt to get myself on multiple local television and radio stations, bringing tens of thousands of visitors to the blog, which just happened to include predominantly displayed ads for all of my products. I'll explain that strategy in detail in Chapter 17.

What blogging software do I use, you may ask?

For me, it's Wordpress. Wordpress is the premier blogging platform. It's stable, it's secure, and thousands of templates, themes, and plug-ins (software goodies) are available, mostly for free, that can give your blog practically any look and functionality you want. Wordpress is so good that it's used by serious heavy hitters. Many major news outlets use Wordpress for their blogs. Even the official White House web site (whitehouse.gov) is a Wordpress blog.

You can either have a hosted blog on the Wordpress servers, or host your blog directly on your own hosting account. I chose the latter, mostly because I have my own powerful web servers that can handle the load, and I can customize it to my heart's extent, but using a blog hosted with Wordpress is fine too. It's free, and a great choice if you can't be bothered with installing Wordpress on your own hosting account. However, hosting the blog yourself will always give you more power and flexibility, so I'd recommend having someone do it for you for a small fee if you're not inclined to do so.

Once you have a basic Wordpress blog set up, the next step is to search for "Wordpress themes." You will found thousands, some free, some paid. Choose one and install it on your blog, or have it installed for you.

Finally, plug-ins are where the real power of Wordpress lies, and are my favorite part of it. Plug-ins allow you to have any capability—and I mean any—that you may want on your site.

Just in case you're wondering, here is the specific list of plug-ins I use on all of my blogs, and that you'll want to check out as well in order to maximize your results (you can find them all, and many more, by searching for "Wordpress plug-ins" online).

- ShareThis. ShareThis is the one plug-in you must have if you could only choose one. It allows readers to e-mail posts and articles to their friends, as well as automatically posting them on their Facebook and other pages. The "Share" button will appear on every blog page and at the end of every post. This is how you grow your readership virally and rapidly expand your audience. Another beautiful thing about ShareThis is that it now allows you to post an article from your blog to a social site, such as Facebook, with just one click. Then, when the post shows prominently on your Facebook (or other) wall, people will click on it, driving more traffic and more sends.

- All-In-One SEO Pack. This plug-in automatically rewrites titles and optimizes your blog for the highest possible rankings in search engine results.
- CommentLuv. Comments are the key to building interactivity, and return visits, to your blog. How many times have you commented on a blog and returned several times to see what others had to say about your thoughts? CommentLuv encourages people to post comments by automatically adding a link from the commenter's own blog, which will give them more traffic and visitors. This is the beauty of blogging—you succeed by including others and helping them out with links, unlike other marketing arenas that are competitive and exclusive.
- Google XML Sitemaps. Have you ever searched online and noticed those results where the site's various pages appear as smaller links beneath the main link? That's called a sitemap, and this plug-in automatically creates one for your blog.
- Reveal IDs for Wordpress Admin. This plug-in doesn't generate traffic, but rather makes administering your blog a lot easier. It assigns ID numbers to every category, page, and more on your blog, making it far easier to post in the correct categories, arrange them on your site, and so on.
- Secure and Accessible PHP Contact Form. This simply adds a contact form to your site's "Contact Us" page, something that is not included in the default Wordpress installation.
- Smart YouTube. This plug-in allows you to add YouTube videos to your blog posts without the complicated embed code; instead, you simply use the URL of the YouTube video itself.
- WordPress.com Stats. This is a biggie: This plug-in provides you with full traffic stats, referring web sites, search engine keywords that brought people to your site, and more. It's key if you not only want to know how many visitors you're getting and which posts and search results are attracting them, but also if you want to optimize your content to maximize the traffic you get.

Those are the big ones. You will certainly find many more plug-ins that you'll want, depending on your personal whims and desires.

One final note on setting up your blog: Search for and make a list of blogs that are related to your topic and, in particular, the ones getting a lot of traffic or run by well-known people. Add a link to their blog in your Blogroll (a list of links to other sites that appear on your blog's homepage, in the sidebar) and many will reciprocate, bringing you massive traffic as well.

13

PODCASTING TO CREATE BUZZ

Podcasting.

Like blogging, it's become both a cornerstone and a centerpiece of the New Media.

Most people I speak with have no idea exactly what podcasting is, nor how much power it can give you. The majority of salespeople and business owners I work with assume that podcasting involves recording and uploading an MP3 audio file to some obscure directory that only total propellor-heads ever visit.

That is absolutely not the case!

For the most part, I don't even bother with uploading my podcasts to endless directories.

The only one I really care much about is Apple's iTunes.

Yes, that's correct. You can record a podcast—even an ongoing radio show with regular episodes—and have it added to the iTunes store, where people can access and download it for free, hugely promoting yourself and your business.

Not only will your podcast appear in the iTunes store—complete with whatever photo or logo you choose to upload—but it can easily be found by users who search for topics they're interested in. And with tens of millions of users—iTunes sells more than five million songs *every day*—it's sure to bring you significant traffic and exposure. In fact, in the "How did you hear about us?" form on all of my checkout pages, iTunes comes up very frequently.

And, despite all this, relatively few people are taking advantage of it. The window is still open to begin podcasting today and take advantage of the user volume. And, since user volume continues to grow rapidly, the window of opportunity will probably be open far longer than we can predict.

I heard a story on the radio not too long ago about an attorney who started a free podcast providing answers to common legal questions, added it to the iTunes directory, and it attracted such a huge audience that he is now a multimillionaire. Yes, his law practice grew *that* much as a result of podcasting on iTunes! I thought I'd let you know in case you're one of those skeptics who thinks "That won't work for me." You'd be amazed at how often I hear those words, despite the fact that people everywhere are proving daily that these strategies will work for anyone.

The next question I usually hear is, "What on earth should I talk about?" That's easy: Provide useful, informative information that is relevant to your target audience, just as the attorney did. In my sales podcasts, I provide sales tips. In my marketing podcasts I provide marketing tips (along with teasers to buy my products). Home improvement contractors give home improvement tips and answer questions from listeners. I learned how to get a burn mark out of one of my expensive suits on a dry cleaner's podcast.

Yes, a dry cleaner.

I told you this applies to anyone and everyone. There are tons of fitness podcasts. Yoga podcasts. Again, anything you can think of is out there.

How to get started?

That depends on what computer platform you use. If you have an Apple Mac computer that is no more than about four years old, you're in luck, because all new Macs come with professional podcasting software preinstalled at the factory (it's called GarageBand, to be specific).

If you're using a Windows PC, there is no one standard software package and the choices are always changing and growing, so my best advice would be to search online, read reviews, and choose a software package that suits you. Just make sure it includes sound loops, so you can add those professional-sounding radio talk show intro and exit clips, making you sound like you're in a professional radio studio.

On that note, you do need to sound professional—your computer's built-in microphone absolutely will not do. On the other hand, you don't need to spend hundreds of dollars on a professional radio microphone and all the hardware you will need to interface it into your computer. I personally use a Logitech USB headset that costs about $50 and plugs right into my computer's USB port, and provides excellent, professional sound quality. They are available at just about any computer or office supply store. Just be sure to stay around the $50 range. The cheaper ones available for about $20 won't cut it.

Also, when it comes to sound, if you're in a room with a lot of hard objects and/or hard walls, you will get a lot of echo, which again will sound unprofessional. When I was still working from home a few years ago, I simply put some pillows and blankets on the hard desktop surfaces surrounding my computer to reduce echo. If you're using a laptop and work from home, a bedroom is a great place because all the bedding absorbs sound.

The next thing you'll need is a blog to host your podcast content. The way iTunes works, you set up a blog first, upload your first podcast, and then submit your blog address to iTunes (go to Podcast Directory in iTunes and then Submit A Podcast). And, find a free podcast hosting service. That's a better idea than paying for storage space, and hosting the content on your own hosting account could potentially slow it down due to the large file sizes.

There are a lot of technical details I don't want to bore you with here, so for full instructions and tutorials on creating your first iTunes podcast, see NeverColdCallBook.com.

Once your podcast is live, which can take up to a week or longer because someone at iTunes manually approves every new submission, you'll have a powerful new tool you can send to your e-mail list, post on your blog(s), add to your Twitter profile, business cards, and much more. Because iTunes gives you a long, cryptic link to your podcast, what I do is add an iTunes folder to my web site and redirect it to that link, for example, NeverCold-Call.com/itunes. This makes promoting your podcast much easier.

One final note: Whether you're doing a short two-minute podcast or a much longer radio show format, promote loud and clear, in between the informative content, of course. Most of my podcasts are short-form, so I end them with, "To learn more and download ten free chapters of my home study course, visit NeverColdCall.com. Thanks for listening and talk to you soon!"

Podcasting is a powerful and effective tool to spread the word and get people talking about you, much the same as a real talk radio program creates buzz and talk about the host. It's a must-have for anyone who wants huge success online so get to it!

14

VODCASTING TO
CREATE BUZZ

Vodcasting—funny sounding word, isn't it?

Vodcasting is simply an abbreviated term for video podcasting.

Yes, in addition to podcasting, there's vodcasting. In fact, as of now, my video podcasts bring me even more traffic than my regular audio podcasts.

That's the good news. The bad news is that it's far more involved to create a high-quality vodcast than it is to create a professional podcast.

And mark my words: Throwing poor-quality video up on the Internet is not going to help you. In fact, when I first began adding video to my web sites, I found that adding low-quality video from a cheap consumer camcorder didn't help me at all. In fact, it *hurt* my results. I use a short video introduction to my home page at NeverColdCall.com. Although the high-quality video that exists there now nearly doubled my opt-in rate, that first low-quality video was even worse than having none on the page.

I continue to be amazed at how many marketers are still using lousy webcam video on home pages. Anytime a self-proclaimed guru insists that his low-quality video is helping things, ask him if he has scientifically split-tested it and has statistically significant results to prove that it's working.

If he doesn't, move on. The common myth in the Internet marketing world is that *any* video is better than no video, but that's simply not the case.

Getting back on topic here—vodcasting—what vodcasting does (or any professional-quality video does) is create the illusion that you are spending tens of thousands of dollars to have professional video produced, possibly even in a professional studio, and therefore you must already be highly successful and wealthy.

Perception is everything in marketing. Everything. By creating the perception that you're already at that level, you are automatically more desirable than your competitors.

And the best part is that it's all totally honest and aboveboard. You're not lying to or misleading anyone. All you're doing is a good job of creating video, and nearly everyone will assume you must have spent big bucks on it.

Now, as I've said, it isn't as easy to pull off as a great podcast. Here's what goes into creating pro video:

- High-quality camera
- Audio
- Lighting
- Background
- Editing and processing

If you're an Apple Mac user, you're in luck again. Macs come preloaded with iMovie HD, professional-quality production software that you can use to very easily create professional level video for your vodcast.

If you're a Windows PC user, it's up to you to find something that suits your price range and is well reviewed. Sony Vegas is the software of choice for most marketers I know who are putting out high-quality content.

Next is a good camera. Just a few years ago, consumer camcorders didn't cut it. Now, there are many out there that will do a very impressive job and even rival some professional studio cameras. The Canon HV30 is a great choice. At this time it's one of the top camcorders under $1,000 out there, it's extremely compact, and it even records in high definition.

For a bit less, you can track down a standard definition camcorder, like the Panasonic PV-GS500 (no longer produced but still in stock at many retailers and easily obtained on the secondhand market). This camera, with sufficient lighting, can produce near broadcast quality video, although you can't create believable green screen footage with it.

In looking for a camera, doing research and reading reviews will be a good idea. Amazon.com is a great source of reviews, as well as CNET.com.

Next, you need good audio. Using the camera's built-in microphone is a bad idea. Very bad.

When I first began experimenting with video, I posted clips on professional video forums. The feedback I consistently got was: "Before you work on your video quality, you need to do something about your audio. It sounds awful."

The issue is that the built-in microphone isn't directional, it picks up background noise, and especially picks up echo. What you need instead is an external directional microphone that mounts on the camera (known as a "shotgun"), or, better yet, a wireless lapel microphone. (I'm not going to go into recommendations here, but use the link at the end of this chapter to learn more.)

Now comes the most important part of all: lighting. Great lighting will make footage from a cheap camcorder look good, and poor lighting will make a $20,000 professional camera look like garbage.

The good news, though, is that you don't have to spend a lot of money on professional lighting if you don't want to. You can rig up cheap worklights to perform as needed. Again, more on that in the link at the end of this chapter.

On backgrounds, the good news here is that you can be very flexible and use pretty much whatever you want. I sometimes shoot video sitting at my desk, sometimes in front of a plain black background, and sometimes in front of a green screen, giving me the availability to key out the green and insert any background image I want, usually a professional news studio as is the case on NeverColdCall.com

Green screen techniques (known to professionals as chroma-key) are again beyond the scope of this book, so check out the link.

As to content, again stick with useful, informative tips that will benefit your audience. And keep the information short and sweet. Video files are large and some users may lack the bandwidth and hard drive space for huge video files. I restrict mine to no longer than three or four minutes, in which I'll provide some useful tips and hints, ending with a call to action to visit my site and get the free download. I also prominently display the web address at the bottom of the screen for the full length of the video because, after all, the whole point of this is getting visitors and opt-ins to our web sites.

As promised, here's the link containing all the details, technical information, product recommendations, and more: NeverColdCallBook.com.

15

Tweeting to Create Buzz and Build a Following

Twitter is a relatively new, and wildly popular, element of social media that has recently achieved mainstream status—television stations, celebrities, and prime-time shows are using Twitter.

Marketers are using Twitter as a powerful addition to an e-mail list to give interested people a way to sign up and get information and updates, without subscribing to an e-mail newsletter.

Businesses are using Twitter to keep customers updated, communicate important updates, and more.

While it may appear to be just an amusing tool to keep in touch with friends, Twitter has great potential to virally grow your following.

First of all, go to Twitter.com and register. Choose a username that's relatively short and easy and that is identifiable as you.

Next, complete your profile, and include in the home page field whatever site you want people ultimately to land on.

Now that you're up and running, you can begin posting updates, a.k.a. "tweets," follow other people, and get others to follow you.

Growing a large list of followers is what you want to do to make the most of Twitter.

When it comes to getting followers, there are a couple of schools of thought. Many people are using software scripts that automatically follow someone who follows you, and then unfollows that person shortly thereafter. The idea is to build a massive list of followers for yourself without having to wade through all of their tweets when looking for the ones you really want to read.

I don't like this.

Getting someone to follow you with the promise of following him back, then suddenly unfollowing him, doesn't seem ethical to me. In essence, you've lied.

I grow my list of followers primarily by including "Follow me on Twitter" links and icons on my various sites and blogs, adding the link to e-mail signatures, including on my support ticket system, and by old-fashioned word of mouth.

In using Twitter, I also don't spam it. Many marketers who attempt to use Twitter send out endless promotions, product launches, links to buy something, and so on. While it's fine to use Twitter to promote—after all, that's why it's included in this book—using it solely as a promotional tool is a mistake.

The reason is that people like to see the personal side of those they admire. That's why there's such a fascination with the private lives of celebrities. In reality, most aren't particularly interesting, but people crave to know what their favorite movie star, singer, or author happens to be doing at any given moment.

So, to satisfy that, I frequently post tweets (usually from my iPhone) telling the world what I'm up to. If I'm getting my car washed, I'll tweet it. If I just watched a great movie, I'll tweet it. If something is annoying me, I'll tweet it.

I also tweet about hobbies, and about current events and politics, because those things interest me.

Twitter, in that fashion, lets people get to me. People send replies to my tweets, and I try to respond to as many of those as possible.

What Twitter really does is build and strengthen a personal connection between my followers and myself, and great marketers are made by the strong relationships they have with their followers.

Upping the ante, the next step in gaining exposure is something called *hashtags*. Hashtags are a way to create groupings on Twitter with people who aren't necessarily your followers, though they can be. Usually it's a diverse group from all backgrounds.

Adding your tweets to groupings is simple: Somewhere in your tweet, you type the grouping's name, immediately preceded by the pound (#) sign. For example, if I wanted to add a tweet to a group entitled "sales," it would look like this:

> **FrankRumbauskas** *My new book is out today, order it on Amazon and get tons of free bonuses! #sales*

That "#sales" at the end is what adds my tweet to the "sales" group.

In order to take advantage of hashtags, you must first add them to your account by going to Twitter.com/hashtags, and clicking the "Follow" button on that page.

The real power of hashtags is getting exposure far beyond your immediate group of followers. People who like your tweets in different groups will follow you. People who follow them will see you in their list of people they follow, and they'll follow you as well. And on and on it goes—classic viral marketing.

Finally, there is the re-tweet. A re-tweet is simply when someone likes your tweet enough to copy and paste it into her own Twitter box, and resend it from her account. Re-tweets are not a formal part of the Twitter system; they are only identifiable by the letters "RT" at the beginning of the tweet.

Sign up for Twitter and begin using it immediately to build your following and grow your business. For more resources on how to get the most from Twitter, along with an up-to-date list of features that are always changing, see NeverColdCallBook.com.

16

SATIRE, COMEDY, AND PUBLICITY STUNTS TO STAND OUT AND ATTRACT ATTENTION

Ahh, satire, comedy, and publicity stunts—some of my favorite buzz-building techniques!

I mentioned in an earlier chapter that I had used a satire site a few years ago to build a tremendous amount of buzz, resulting in local television and radio appearances—and radio hosts continuing to talk about it for months after. That, in turn, drove tens of thousands of people to the web site, which just happened to contain ads for my real web sites.

With the sheer amount of traffic I received (over three thousand new visitors a day for quite a long time), enough people clicked on my ads and bought my products to put thousands of dollars in my pocket for something that was a lot of fun and got me bragging rights for being on television.

Here are the details:

I was living in Scottsdale, Arizona, a suburb of Phoenix, at the time. If you live or have ever lived there—and please don't take offense if you do—Scottsdale is one of the most pretentious places in the United States. If you're a down-to-earth, laid-back person like me, you get the impression that everyone around you has the singular goal in life to impress others with an appearance of wealth, even if he or she flips burgers at McDonald's for a living.

One night I was out on a date with someone who was brand-new to Phoenix and thought I was exaggerating in describing Scottsdale to her. To prove it, we went out to a Scottsdale bar and I challenged her to go up to any single guy, start a conversation, and mention that she'd recently moved from the New York City area. I told her that he'd respond by saying he was just there, or has a place there, or goes there all the time.

She did it, mentioned that she'd just moved to Arizona from New York, and without missing a beat, he said, "Oh, I was just in Manhattan for a week playing golf."

Manhattan as a golf destination? Only in Scottsdale.

It's full of the most self-absorbed people I've ever met or even heard of. I never met most of my neighbors, who would come home, pull the car into the garage, and immediately close the door before having to see or talk to anyone.

The one time I rang a neighbor's doorbell in the evening to let him know he'd left his garage door open, he mumbled, "Oh, okay, thanks" before slamming the door shut.

If you smile and say hi to a stranger, they say nothing in return and look at you like you're a three-headed alien.

Almost every woman you see has bleached blonde hair. Most are "enhanced"—in fact, Scottsdale, with a population of just over 200,000, has almost as many "surgically enhanced" women as Los Angeles with 3.9 million people. This suburb of Phoenix comes in at #3 nationwide, with Miami taking the #2 slot.

On top of all that, the local government is extremely corrupt, as is the police department, which routinely abuses the DUI and speed laws to make questionable arrests and issue ridiculous tickets, like driving one mph above the speed limit.

I think you get the point by now.

As you can guess, those of us who got sick of this endless nonsense really came to dislike living in Scottsdale. Day after day I heard people saying, "I wish I could just vent and get this frustration off my shoulders. Something to blow off steam from the stress of being around these idiots, day after day."

In response, I put up a web site called Scottsdale Sucks.

It was an overnight sensation.

I don't even post there anymore and yet there are new comments added every day, from people writing things like "I moved here X number of years ago and could not believe it. Thank you for stating the truth and giving me a place to vent!"

Once I saw the attention it was getting, the ads went up!

Radio morning shows began talking about it, saying that it's pretty brutal but all true.

Then the TV stations came calling and interviewed me on live television. That's what got the ball rolling big-time and got the traffic pouring in.

Another example of an effective publicity stunt—an offline one—was done by my friend, Dr. Joe Vitale, who you may know from the hit movie *The Secret*. Joe put together the Canine Concert a few years ago in Austin, Texas.

The Canine Concert consisted of musicians playing music at very high frequencies that only dogs can hear, as is the case with a dog whistle.

The idea was so unusual that it attracted huge amounts of attention and publicity. Local media and television were in attendance.

There was even a protester holding a sign that read, "Canine Concert Is Unfair To Cats!"

Why did Joe go to all this trouble?

To launch his new book, *There's A Customer Born Every Minute* (John Wiley & Sons, 2006), based on the teachings of P. T. Barnum and how one can apply them to marketing.

And yes, there was even a man playing the part of Mr. Barnum, complete with clothing from that era.

Predictably, the major media exposure sold a ton of books for Joe.

And that's part of the reason why you should begin brainstorming publicity stunts.

Yes, they can bring a lot of traffic to your for-profit web sites. But they also attract media very easily—far more easily than using press releases and other strategies.

The trick, though, is to have a reason for the publicity stunt. If Joe Vitale had done the Canine Concert without any end goal in mind, it would have attracted just as much media, but it wouldn't have sold any books or put any money into his pocket.

Formulating a stunt like Joe's isn't hard to do. As a marketing guy, he chose P. T. Barnum as his symbol. A lawyer might use Abe Lincoln; a banker, J. P. Morgan. And so on.

And of course, controversial blogging is a lot faster and easier to do right now. These days, you can poke fun at just about anything you want to. Keep it cutting-edge and controversial, which is the key to making it go viral.

Political opinions are another way to go, as long as you're not afraid of offending anyone. In my own experience of doing some political blogging and tweeting, the few people I lose as potential customers are far offset by the many people who come to love me because they agree with me. So, in the end, I gain a lot of net new customers.

The choice is all yours. Think of a controversial topic you care about, or create a live stunt as Joe did, and use it to create big buzz and get easy media exposure.

17

THE ULTIMATE BUZZ-BUILDER: YOUR OWN SOCIAL NETWORK

By now, you've certainly heard all about social networking. It's in the news all the time and has become a household term.

You've probably also used social networking yourself on sites like Facebook or MySpace. Or, perhaps you've used a professional social networking site like LinkedIn to network and make connections.

Social networking is now a part of life, and any marketer who wants to achieve big results is using it.

There are several ways to engage social networking. Here is a list of the most common, from least to most powerful.

- Joining social networks. If you're a member of Facebook or any other popular social networking site, you've already completed this most basic step. Becoming a member of social networking sites lets people easily find you (reconnecting with lost friends and schoolmates is fun), allows you to make many new friends, is a great way to find new business networking contacts, and by completing your profile(s) thoroughly, it allows people with similar interests and business goals to find you. It's quick, easy, and free to join any of these sites—I suggest joining them all. When you do, be sure to use the "invite my friends" feature, sending it out to your entire e-mail address book. By doing so, you make yourself more visible, and you exponentially multiply the numbers of new friends you'll make.

- Promoting your business with social networking sites. This is a gray area and a bit of a touchy subject. Many sites, such as MySpace, prohibit explicit business marketing in most cases. So, before you put up a page under your business name or web address on every site, check out its terms. I'm not going to list them here because things change all the time and the information could potentially be outdated by the time you get this book, so do your research online and find out. As before, if you use this idea, be sure to invite your full address book(s) in order to maximize your reach and results.

- Creating a fan page. This is where the real fun begins. By creating a fan page on a site like Facebook, you accomplish several things. First of all, you create a sort of celebrity status for yourself. Remember that most people who use these sites aren't students of Internet marketing as you and I are. Instead, they know little about it and probably have no idea that anyone can create a fan page. As a result, they are going to assume that you are someone important. This gives you the automatic status and authority that bring instant credibility and, in turn, earn the respect and trust of potential customers. Make sure you invite your entire network and address book(s) to join your fan club.

- Facebook advertising. At the time of this writing, Facebook has been offering paid advertising (at very low cost) and I've been using it myself for quite a while. Recently, Facebook has added "social features" to their advertising platform. Integrating your ads with your fan page is my favorite feature. Here's how it works: After setting up your ads, you click to add social features to one or more of them. Then, anytime someone joins your fan page, and your fan page appears in their profile's fan page list, your ad is automatically inserted into it. This really boosts click-through rate and traffic from those ads. In addition, because people of similar backgrounds and similar careers tend to be friends online more often than not, it will create more targeted traffic—and therefore increase your return on investment—to a large degree. One warning: If you decide to use Facebook advertising, regardless of whether or not you include the social features, be sure to make your ad(s) *very* targeted. With the sheer number of users on Facebook, you'll get tons and tons of irrelevant clicks that will waste a lot of your money if you don't target them. I recommend starting with extremely highly targeted ads, and gradually loosen them up while monitoring your spending.

- Your own social network. This is the most powerful of all techniques, and the one we'll focus on for the remainder of this chapter.

The only thing better than using a public social network is creating your own.

It makes you the focus and the center of the site—the entire reason for the site's existence.

When you create a social network that is focused entirely on you or your business, you not only give yourself a huge level of respect and visibility, but you engage powerful viral marketing tools available nowhere else.

I maintain a social network for salespeople called Recession Crusher.com. Even though it's free for users—and costs me almost nothing to operate, just a tiny fee each month to remove third-party advertising and use my own domain name—it provides tremendous value to members and really gives them a lot, all at zero cost.

Members get their own blog. There are discussion forums, groups (that anyone can create), tons of videos (both from myself as well as other members), photo galleries, a member directory, and a download page full of high value content authored by me.

There is also full-featured social networking. Members love it because they're all salespeople or small business owners who face the same challenges. They can make new friends with like-minded people, create alliances and joint ventures, share ideas and techniques, and much more. It's really worth gold to any salesperson or marketer who takes advantage of it.

That's what members get. Now, let's talk about what I get out of it.

Let's start with the sign-up process. A new member finds the site, either through my newsletter, through an invitation from an existing member, or via an online search.

After landing on the page, the visitor finds lots of cool and valuable stuff in plain view, but quickly gets a prompt to register before gaining access to any of it. Since registration is free, most people do it.

Immediately upon registering, a blank "Tell Us About You" page is presented that must be completed before full access is granted (as administrator, I created all of the questions on that page). After the page is completed and the user submits it, it autopopulates the person's blog page, so it's complete and ready to go immediately. There's no more work for the user to do. He can also upload his photos, videos, and more.

After that, the new and usually excited member is presented with—you guessed it—a tell-a-friend page. This one is unusually effective, because instead of telling his friends about my products, he is inviting them to join his social network and to view his personal blog page.

And for me, that's the best part, because it is viral marketing on autopilot. I do absolutely nothing to grow and promote the site—members do all of that for me.

Naturally, once users are inside the site, they are sending items to friends, inviting new friends to their network, downloading great free content, participating in groups and discussion forums, watching videos, and so much more.

The best part is that they're learning and making new connections with like-minded people, and profiting from it all. I've always said the people who buy my NeverColdCall.com products and then get involved with the groups and forums are the ones who profit the most from it.

At this point, I know exactly what you're thinking: This probably cost me a small fortune to have developed, probably thousands of dollars at a minimum.

You couldn't be more wrong—it's all free!

My network is based on Ning.com, a free social networking platform. Okay, so I pay $40 a month to remove the Google AdWords ads from the page and to use my own domain name (RecessionCrusher.com instead of RecessionCrusher.Ning.com), but 40 bucks is a pittance compared to the money the site makes for me, let alone the tremendous value it gives to members. And that makes me feel great.

Do this right now: Go to Ning.com and sign up for your free account. Start your own social network, choose a template (or customize the look and feel and colors on your own). and begin profiting from this amazing new platform.

In addition to Ning, there are a few alternatives that are a bit more difficult to set up, but you might want to take a look at them. First, there's a new system available for Wordpress Multi-User called BuddyPress. If you're a little more advanced than the average person, or if you have access to a web developer to set it up for you, this is an even better alternative than Ning. Since it resides on your own hosting account, you have complete control over it, and you have all the advantages of the amazing flexible and ever-improving Wordpress platform.

Also, Google has recently introduced Google Friend Connect. What it does is allow you to register any site with Google, and then add sign-up forms and "widgets" to the site pages, giving members the ability to enjoy social networking features on a site that is not necessarily designed nor equipped for social networking.

For more detailed information on Ning, BuddyPress, Google Friend Connect, and other aspects of social networking, see NeverColdCallBook.com.

Part IV

Generating Highly Targeted, High-Value Traffic

18

A Brief Background on Traffic Generation and Search Engines

Naturally, getting traffic to your web site is necessary to get the ball rolling in Internet marketing. Nobody is going to sign up for your e-mail list, and nobody is going to buy your products, unless and until they visit your site.

Keep in mind, though, that getting traffic is not necessarily *the* most important part of Internet marketing. There is a lot more that goes into it because, after all, what good is traffic if it doesn't convert? (*Convert* is Internet marketing lingo for making a sale, or *converting* a prospect into a customer.)

With that in mind, a brief discussion on search engines is in order.

At this point, you've learned about various methods of getting traffic to your site, some or all of which you may have never known existed.

That's why you should take the concept that search engine optimization (SEO) is a must for your business with a grain of salt.

It's a common misconception among inexperienced marketers that the key to success is getting your web site listed very high, if not at the top, of search engine rankings. And there's good reason for it. It makes sense to have your site at the top of Google rankings, right? You'll have seemingly endless traffic and income if you can pull it off, right?

Not necessarily.

While I'm sure there really are people who can manage to make a nice income from getting to #1 on Google with their key search phrase, it certainly didn't turn out that way for me. After lots of time and effort, I got NeverColdCall.com to #1 on Google for the phrase "cold calling," and I sat back and waited for the big killing to come in.

It never did.

While I generate thousands of new visitors to my site every day using some methods I've already told you about, being #1 on Google for "cold calling" brought me an average of 100 new visitors per day, with an average of a whopping zero percent buying the product.

How is that possible?

In reality, that is the case more often than not.

It is for that reason that I personally do not bother with SEO, and why you won't find it taught in this book. Yes, that's correct: As a top marketer, I don't waste my time on SEO.

The reasons are numerous. Here is a partial list of why SEO usually doesn't work.

- Optimizing a site to attain #1 ranking in Google for one specific search phrase or keyword is almost always counter-productive. The reason is that literally *thousands* of search term combinations bring quality traffic to my sites. Cold calling really doesn't bring me anywhere near as much traffic as do variations and totally unrelated terms—everything from "insurance cold calling" to "how to sell whole life insurance to parents in Nevada." Avoid optimizing a site for a single search phrase since all that does is potentially shut out other search phrases that will not only generate traffic but convert to sales as well.

- Optimizing a site for SEO will almost certainly hurt the site's opt-in and conversion rates. Effective copy that gets people to sign up and subsequently buy is *far* more important than copy that only aims to please the search engines. The issue here is that changing your site's copy and content to attain a high ranking on Google is going to completely change what you have now, and for the worse. If your site's copy and content are written to generate sales—as they should be—you'll want to keep them that way. Don't go messing them up or taking the advice of an SEO consultant. In sales, the goal is to *make a sale*, not get the most appointments. The same is true with Internet marketing—your goal is to *generate sales*, not to get the maximum number of site visitors. What good is a visitor who finds you on Google but who doesn't buy because your sales copy is weak?

- Natural (or organic) search engine traffic doesn't convert nearly as well as more targeted traffic, such as traffic from podcasts, YouTube, pay-per-click marketing, and others. Remember I said that exactly zero percent of my organic search visitors ever bought anything? The reason is that visitors who find you through a press release, article, podcast, or video are already partially presold. They're already interested in you and what you have to say, and therefore they're more predisposed to buy than someone who clicks on nothing more than a search result. In the case of pay-per-click marketing, it converts much better for two reasons: First, people who are ready to buy with a credit card in hand tend to gravitate toward the paid search listing results rather than the natural listings. This is because many of the natural results are purely informational, while the paid results are clearly selling a product that the prospect is looking for (this goes back to the basic rule in sales of attracting people who are ready, willing, and able to buy, instead of lookers and time-wasters). Second, in pay-per-click marketing, you can experiment with and test different ad headlines and copy to find the ones that are most effective, while with natural results you're stuck with what the Google algorithm comes up with. Also, you can track and measure results with pay-per-click marketing to an extremely precise degree and make changes for the maximum end result.

- Google and other search engines change their algorithms frequently and without warning. There is little benefit to spending a lot of time, money, or both to get to the top of Google, just to have them change their formula and wipe your site from the front page of search results entirely. And guess what? It happens all the time. Google and other search engines know that SEO consultants are always looking for new ways to game the system, and every time that happens, Google changes their algorithm accordingly, inevitably throwing search results off across the board.

- And finally, SEO is time-intensive. There are much better ways to invest your time that will get you far better results than messing with search engines and hoping to get something out of it—because SEO is far from a precise science, and may not work for you even if you do everything right.

Don't get me wrong: I do get tons of traffic via the search engines, and so will you, but not with SEO. My articles appear in search results. So do all of my YouTube videos and press releases. Blog posts, forum posts, and more all appear in search engines, eventually bringing people to my site—and usually partially sold on me by the time they get there.

Now promise me—and yourself—that you won't get sucked into the SEO trap! It's just not worth it.

19

YOUR E-MAIL LIST: YOUR MOST PRECIOUS ONLINE ASSET

I'm sure by now you've heard the saying, "The money is in the list."

I'm here to tell you it's true. Very true. Unlike SEO, building a large e-mail list, building a relationship with your list, and keeping your subscribers onboard—you won't get very far if people are unsubscribing—is the engine that powers an Internet marketing empire.

Trying to run an online business without a powerful lead-capture mechanism and e-mail follow-up system is right up there with a cold call: It's a single moment in time that fails to build a relationship and disappears instantly. One of the biggest problems with cold calling is that you have only a minute or two to get the prospect interested and to move the sales process forward by securing an appointment. This is ineffective because if you don't get the prospect interested instantly, the opportunity is forever lost and you must move on to the next person. This is why cold calling has a dismal success rate and why most salespeople who try to rely on it fail.

The same is true for a home page that has any other purpose than to get the new visitor to sign up for your e-mail newsletter.

Your web site's goal with any new visitor is not to make a sale.

Let me repeat that: The goal of your site's home page, when receiving a new visitor, is *not to make sale.*

It is to capture a new lead.

If you take a look at the home page on NeverColdCall.com, you won't see any mention of buying my product, nor will you see any sales pitch for it. There's a sales pitch on the page all right, but it's not to buy my product. It's to get a free download—the first 10 chapters of the book portion of the package—in exchange for giving me your name and e-mail address.

At that point, new visitors may not even know that they're downloading a free sample—a teaser, if you will—of a product I'm going to ask them to buy later. They just see a 10-chapter free download of a book that claims to solve one of their problems, that of generating leads without the misery of cold calling, and they get excited about it. There are even a few testimonials on the page, for both the newsletter and the book.

Why is this so important?

First of all, as I've said, you're out to get a lead. Capturing a lead does several things. It gives you the opportunity to win a potential customer over time. Most people aren't going to buy on the initial visit, because they know the Internet is full of scam artists and you need first to earn their trust. Many people will have unanswered questions or concerns that will be answered in your newsletters. Others will only buy after they've heard some impressive testimonials and success stories from happy customers, again delivered in your newsletter.

Second, capturing a lead creates a long-term relationship. Let's say someone does buy your product on their first visit to your site. Does this mean you're done with them? Of course not! As the line from the famous (or infamous) movie *Glengarry Glen Ross* goes, "You don't sell a guy a car. You sell him five cars over fifteen years."

It's all about long-term value; customers for life, if you will. I know it works because the gentleman I buy my cars from practices it. For a time he was the number one Jaguar salesman in the *world,* and now is in the top 1 percent of Mercedes-Benz salesmen, again, in the world! And he sells his cars in Phoenix, Arizona—certainly not the largest or wealthiest market in the United States or the world.

And that is where your relationship with your list comes in.

I first heard Jeff Walker say, "The real money isn't in your list but in your relationship with your list." That was a few years ago, and letting it sink in, I realized that I had indeed built a strong relationship with my subscribers. I provide them with what they want in my newsletter, I convey enough personality to engage them, and I don't bombard them with useless and annoying sales pitches. Most importantly, I don't sell their e-mail addresses, nor do I sell advertising in the newsletter.

As Van Halen said, "It's mine, all mine."

The key to building a strong relationship with your list is to provide only useful, informative content in your newsletter. Content is king. Remember that.

My newsletters go out weekly, alternating between a straightforward newsletter one week and a mailbag question and answer format the alternate week.

In my straightforward newsletters, I choose a topic that's of concern or interest to salespeople and small business owners, or sometimes a current concern such as the economy, and write an e-mail addressing it. I'm essentially writing an article, but for use as that week's newsletter instead.

In my mailbags I post actual e-mails that readers have sent in, and follow those with my replies. Most are questions that people want answers to, but I'm always sure to sprinkle in at least one testimonial with the reader telling me how much my product has done for him, and a short reply from me thanking him for the positive comments and congratulating him on his success. This technique is extremely powerful and I typically use testimonials as the first or last item in a mailbag with an average of five letters per issue.

Of course, at the very end of each newsletter is a call to action. If I close a mailbag with a testimonial, it's something to the effect of "If you want to achieve the kind of success that John Doe is enjoying, then you need to buy my home study course right now."

At the end of a regular newsletter, it's more like, "Remember, you can get my full home study course including the book, CDs, and the hundreds of dollars in powerful bonuses and you don't even have to pay me today—you'll have a full 30 days to try it out for free. If you don't like it, send it back and we won't even charge you. Get your copy right now." (Notice I say "get" instead of "buy" or "order"—more on this in the chapter on writing effective copy.)

The key to maintaining a good relationship with your list and to discourage them from unsubscribing is by keeping your sales pitch very low-key and discreet, and making a sales pitch only after you've delivered quality content.

While we're talking about blatant sales pitches, let's touch on third-party and affiliate promotions.

Affiliate promotions are, in most cases, a blatant sales pitch. However, there are ways to do it that won't put your subscribers off.

- Don't promote products that you haven't reviewed yourself. If the product doesn't deliver as promised, you'll have a lot of angry subscribers and you'll only have yourself to blame for not checking it out first.
- Don't promote for anyone who doesn't have a stellar reputation or who is completely unknown. Again, if your customers get ripped off, they're not going to blame the seller—they're going to blame *you* for promoting a ripoff artist.
- Don't promote anything that isn't relevant to your list. If you're a sales author like me, for example, promoting nutritional supplements probably isn't a good idea and would make me look like a spammer to my subscribers.
- Finally, keep the affiliate promotions few and far between. Any more than once or twice a month is going to make you look

like a spammer and will anger a lot of your subscribers, who will immediately unsubscribe.

As you can see, building—and keeping—a large and targeted list is something you simply can't do without in Internet marketing. To learn more, including specific e-mail programs and services that I recommend, along with how to set them up, see NeverColdCallBook.com.

20

INSTANT TRAFFIC: COST-EFFECTIVE PAY-PER-CLICK MARKETING

If you follow me or my blog at all, you know that pay-per-click (PPC) marketing is, by far, my favorite method of generating traffic.

Wait a minute, you might say. Don't all the big-shot Internet marketers badmouth PPC? Don't all the so-called gurus and experts claim that real marketers don't use PPC? That if you know what you're doing, you don't need to buy traffic?

I'm here to tell you it's all rubbish.

First of all, just about every highly successful Internet marketer is using PPC to some degree.

Second, anyone who tells you that you don't need to buy traffic when you can use dozens of other methods to get it for free is an idiot. Here's why: Let's say, for the sake of argument, that you are using every technique in this book, except for PPC, and you're getting 1,000 new visitors a day from it. That's pretty impressive, and for most people with a well-written site and a good offer, five figures per month in income is realistic. For this example, we'll say $15,000 per month.

If you're making that kind of money, and you're happy with it, and you have no ambition or desire to make more money, that's fine. Don't use PPC.

On the other hand, someone who is getting a thousand hits a day from free traffic will easily get at least that much, usually more, from a well-designed PPC campaign. So you have your thousand hits a day, you sign up for Google AdWords, and suddenly you have another thousand hits a day. Since PPC traffic converts better than anything else, you immediately begin making another $20,000 per month, take out $5,000 for the cost of the PPC ads, and suddenly you've doubled your money!

Here's the weakness of the "real marketers don't use PPC" argument: If you're already successful online, and you obviously have something people want to buy, why on earth wouldn't you want to bring your offer to an entirely new audience?

Traffic from PPC is going to come from completely different people than your other traffic sources generate. And, since PPC traffic has proven to convert better than all other forms of traffic—these are people who *want to buy something*, after all—you wind up with an even higher return on investment than before.

There's another side to this story as well. What if you're launching a brand-new business online, or you have an existing business, or are a salesperson who is taking your product online for the first time?

Well, I have news for you: All those methods of generating free traffic may work, but they take a *long time* to work. That's a big problem with free traffic methods. They take a long time to begin working because they're slow, and they partly rely on others to spread the word about you. That's why, in my businesses, I always begin with PPC first, and then, and only then, do I begin spending lots of time on other traffic generation methods.

Look at how my very first Internet business, NeverColdCall.com, started. I created the web site (a lousy web site because I didn't know any better at the time), I created the product in just a few days, and then I signed up for Google AdWords, put in a few keywords and ad variations, and went live.

Thirty minutes later, I had my first sale.

They continued to roll in.

Less than six weeks later, I quit my last job ever, because my Google AdWords campaign was already earning me $6,000 per month in net, passive income.

For the next several months, I tracked, tested, measured, and adjusted my AdWords campaigns. Only then did I even begin exploring ways to get free traffic.

If I'd started with free traffic, like most new marketers do, I probably would have given up and failed. Realistically, it would've taken months to get that first sale, not 30 minutes. I was making good money at my job, and probably I would have scrapped the Internet business and stayed at the job.

Almost seven years later, the thought of having a job absolutely terrifies me. Now that I have my present lifestyle, I cannot imagine anything else.

Now that I've hit you with the hard sell on why you need to use PPC, you have a lot of options. The biggie is Google AdWords. There is also MSN AdCenter, Yahoo Search Marketing, Facebook advertising, and several other smaller choices.

At this time I use Google AdWords for nearly all of my PPC marketing—about 90 percent—with Facebook advertising making up the other 10 percent. Facebook advertising works well but as of now it's hard to target and still rough around the edges.

I no longer use Yahoo Search Marketing nor MSN AdCenter. They're quite user-unfriendly and confusing, and since they bring in only a tiny fraction of the amount of traffic that AdWords does, it's not worth my time to mess with them.

Here's how to get started with AdWords. I'm not going to go into the full technical details here—that would consume half this book—so I'll provide a couple of resources at the end of the chapter instead.

First, you sign up with Google AdWords. Go to adwords.com, register, and sign up for the Standard Edition (Starter Edition doesn't give you full access to all of AdWords' powerful capabilities).

Next, enter an ad. You get 25 characters for the headline and 35 characters per line for the two lines of ad content—counting spaces as characters—so you need to keep it very short, but also powerful and attractive enough to make people click on your ad.

Then, you enter a list of keywords. Keep it simple for now—type in the most common words and phrases people may use to find a product like yours.

After that you will enter a minimum bid. This is the minimum amount you will pay per click. Around $0.25 per click is a good place to start.

Then you'll be asked to enter a daily budget. This is the absolute maximum amount you will spend per day. When you reach this budget, AdWords will automatically shut your campaign(s) down until the next day. When you do this, keep in mind that the lower your budget, the less frequently your ads will show, and you may get little or no traffic, so go high. Don't worry, it's doubtful that you'll ever come anywhere near your daily budget—mine is over $10,000, yet I rarely spend over $500!

At the very end, save your new campaign and ad group.

Following that, find the "Conversion Tracking" option in the top menu bar. There you'll follow a series of steps to generate a couple of code snippets. You'll paste one onto your landing page (or home page) as indicated, and the other goes on your order confirmation, or thank-you page. What this will do is track everything that happens within your campaigns so you can see exactly which combinations of keywords and ad variations are generating sales. Over time you'll gradually increase the bids on effective combinations, while decreasing bids, or even deleting, the ineffective keywords and ads.

Naturally, I've just given you an overly simplified version of AdWords, but it is enough to get you started. The most important part of optimizing AdWords, or any other PPC campaigns, is tracking. That's why I advise you to set up Google Conversion Tracking, because without it or another tracking solution, you'll have no idea what's working or what's not, and you'll probably get a poor return on investment in the end.

For a complete fast-track guide to getting started with Google AdWords, go to AdWordsInsideSecrets.com and get the 10-chapter free download. It will give you everything you need to know to get started. I've also posted more resources on PPC and AdWords at NeverColdCallBook.com.

21

WRITE ARTICLES TO GENERATE TRAFFIC AND BUILD BACKLINKS

I explained the power of writing and uploading high-quality articles back in Chapter 7. The purpose there was, of course, to give you instant and verifiable expert status, and in one case, Expert Author status and online visibility as a recognized expert.

There is another purpose to writing articles; namely, to get people interested in you and clicking through to your web site. In the marketing world, this technique is known as "article marketing."

In article marketing, your goal is to write a high-quality article that is informative and useful to readers, that portrays you as the undisputed expert in your field, and that impresses or interests readers enough so that they click through to your web site. A link to your web site will reside in the bio, or "resource box," at the end of the article.

The key to getting people reading your articles in the first place is to use a title that is enticing, edgy, and controversial, or a combination of all three.

Here are a few examples of edgy article titles I've used in the past to promote NeverColdCall.com.

- The Problem with Cold Calling 2.0 and Other Urban Legends
- The Cold Calling Conspiracy
- The Hidden Cost of Cold Calling
- The Fallacy of Funnels and Forecasts
- Cold Calling's Dark Side

And here are some examples of helpful article titles that entice people to read.

- How to Stop Chasing Prospects Forever
- Keeping Your Sales Team Motivated
- Sales Prospecting for Long-Term Success
- Use Social Dynamics to Control Sales Appointments

As you can see, the titles work. There's nothing boring like "Sales Prospecting Tips"—the titles are unique and specific. They really appeal to someone who is searching for an answer to a particular problem.

Next, your article needs to be effective, informative, and most of all, accurate.

If you're going with an edgy title that piques someone's curiosity, follow through with that in the article. Get the readers excited, fired up, and dying to visit your web site. For example, my best-performing article ever is "The Cold Calling Conspiracy." Salespeople who are fed up with cold calling are instantly drawn to it, and since they're excited to see what I have to say, I keep the edginess up throughout the article, painting a picture of sales managers who require cold calling as evil people in cahoots with the company to screw over the sales reps.

I do this all with full accuracy by explaining how companies do in fact force cold calling on salespeople to reduce or even eliminate their marketing budgets, ultimately putting the expense on the salesperson through increased stress and lower sales volume. So, the article isn't just edgy and controversial, but is also factually accurate.

I typically close such an article with a call to action and an enticement to click on my web site link at the end of the article, such as, "Stop wasting your time and losing money with cold calling, and learn techniques that get real results instead."

Following that is the bio, or resource box. It serves as both a bio and a sales pitch to get people to your web site. The nice thing about sites like EzineArticles.com is that they allow you to enter and save one or more default resource boxes, so with each article submission, you simply choose the one you want. Here's one of mine:

New York Times *best-selling author Frank Rumbauskas has taught tens of thousands of salespeople and small business owners how to stop cold calling and start selling, and he's regularly featured in mainstream media as a top sales expert. To download 10 free chapters of Frank's powerful "Never Cold Call Again" home study course, visit NeverColdCall.com.*

So, rather than a bland paragraph saying Frank is an author and where he's from, there is first a testament to what my materials have done for people, another statement of credibility, and finally, a strong call to action to visit my site.

"To learn more, visit NeverColdCall.com" is weak. "To get 10 free chapters of Frank's powerful home study course," however, is motivating, and it generates traffic and sales. It also gets people on my side ahead of time, partially predisposed to buy before even visiting my site. I've displayed my credibility up-front, and people have instant confidence and trust before they even land on my home page.

To get the most out of article marketing, you'll need to write lots of articles. I find that the only way I get them done is to mark two days per week on my calendar as recurring events and to write and upload a new article on each of those days. After a while, once you have dozens or even hundreds of articles out there, you can back off to once per week or month, but never stop, because articles can get stale in the eyes of search engines over time.

The results of this can be dramatic. I know of people who have written thousands of articles over a period of years, resulting in millions of web site visits and, consequently, millions of dollars in sales.

And this is done just with article marketing, let alone all the other tools you have at your disposal online!

Once you're cranking out articles, it's not enough to upload them to one or just a few sites. You need more exposure, and more backlinks.

Backlinks, quite simply, are links back to your web site. Since each article contains a live link to your site, and because the number of backlinks is one of the top factors that search engines like Google will use to rank you, the more the merrier.

By using a low-cost article distribution service (my personal favorite is ArticleMarketer.com), you can automatically upload each article to literally thousands of article databases. At the time of this writing, ArticleMarketer.com uploads to 3,696 sites. That's nearly *four thousand backlinks* to your site, for each article you write.

While we're on that thought, you may have heard about the evil specter of Google's "duplicate content" rule. Yes, it's real: Posting the identical article on multiple pages will hurt your search ranking; however, it only happens if you post identical content on multiple pages *of the same web site.* So, don't worry about that when it comes to article directories. Having each one of your articles appear on thousands of sites cannot hurt you and will only help you.

The rest is up to you—get started on writing and submitting articles. Check out NeverColdCallBook.com for more tips and secrets to maximizing article marketing results and putting cash in your pocket.

22

How to Build Traffic—and Your List—with Internet Forums

Internet forums are one of those hidden ways to generate traffic, and fast. As is the case with social networking, you can participate either as a member of other forums or as the owner of your own. I'll cover both methods in this chapter.

The fastest and easiest way to get instant, prequalified traffic is to join a forum, create a signature containing a live link to your web site, and start posting and participating in discussions.

Note that some forums prohibit links in signatures. Don't waste your time with these. Spend your time only on the ones that allow links, since bans on links won't get you any traffic, and because those forums are usually run by control freaks who act like dictators and overmoderate the forum. They will ban you the instant they recognize you as an expert who might threaten their authority.

Having gotten that bit of unpleasant business out of the way, search and find forums that are relevant to whatever it is you sell.

For example, in my persona as an Internet marketing expert, I post and participate in discussions on Internet marketing forums. And, to be quite honest, I learn just as much there as I teach, because I am constantly picking up new tips and tricks, enabling my business to grow indefinitely.

On sales forums, I show up as the best-selling sales author, and again, post useful answers and participate in discussions, strictly in the role of helping people rather than trying to sell anything (which would get me banned). People see the "Never Cold Call Again" link in my signature, and, appreciating the free help I've already given, they click through to my web site and buy my products.

More recently I learned that my local bank has a small business forum, which is great for me because it straddles sales, small business, and marketing, meaning I'm relevant to pretty much everyone there. Things got even better when I noticed that not a lot of people were active members of the site, meaning that I could post and it would stay visible for days, yet each individual post gets thousands of views. This allowed me to post and participate complete with my link in my signature, bringing countless new visitors to my site and putting thousands of dollars into my pocket, all for spending a few minutes each day answering questions about sales and marketing.

Before moving forward, I'd like to remind you of the Law of Compensation, which says that there are checks and balances in everything. People who scam others and try to get things for free will eventually pay a price for it, thus balancing the scales of justice. On the other hand, those of us who give and help others freely, with no expectation of anything in return, will benefit greatly as our good deeds come back to us. And, the longer it takes for the payoff to come, the more interest accumulates and the greater our payoff will be.

This is so true in the world of marketing. For example, my social network, RecessionCrusher.com, freely gives away thousands of dollars in products I've created over the years that were quite expensive but that I now let people download for free.

In the world of forums, those of us who freely answer the questions and challenges of others, without selling and without plugging our products, reap great rewards in return. Not only do people click through to our sites, but they talk about us and we become known as great people who can be trusted. Those who get on forums and try to sell are usually banned very quickly, and word spreads that they're opportunists who are only out for themselves.

And, on top of all that, spending time each day helping others for free feels pretty good, too.

Now that you understand the benefits of participating in forums as a helpful member, an even more powerful activity is to run your very own Internet forums.

It's not hard to do—free software such as PHPbb that also has plenty of free templates, themes, and plug-ins available, like Wordpress, can get you started quickly and easily. You can even add PHPbb as a page in your Wordpress site. Or you can put up a free Ning site that has forums built into it. I'll skip all the technical details here—they're posted for you at NeverColdCallBook.com.

At first, running your own forum won't get the immediate results that posting in other busy forums will, *unless* you already have a large list to whom you can announce the forum. Hundred or even thousands of people will sign up immediately and begin posting, or you can post new threads on your forum, closing each one with "Your thoughts?", and getting people posting right away.

The benefits of having your own forum outweigh those of participating on others—though you'll want to continue doing both.

First of all, when you have your own forum and you're the administrator, you're the boss. Being the leader of anything makes people trust and respect you, and it makes you look powerful.

Second, since it's your own forum, you'll place advertisements to visit your main site on the forum's main template, just as I do on my Ning site. It will get new visitors clicking through to your site and eventually buying. You can also set up your forum software to insert ads randomly between posts in a discussion thread.

Third, you'll naturally have your link to your main business site in your signature, and since you'll be participating regularly and posting in threads—giving free help and advice, of course—you'll get plenty of traffic that way while also bolstering your credibility.

The real beauty of having your own forum, though, is that it's human nature to desire to know what others had to say about their posts. Seriously, how many times have you posted in a forum, only to return several more times just to read responses? This is extremely powerful. It gets people returning over and over, and seeing your ads and hearing your message every time.

As you get to know members in your forums, you'll become acquainted with some whom you'll come to trust, and can then appoint as moderator to delete spam posts, remove inappropriate posts, and ban troublemakers from the forum altogether. On one forum in which I'm a moderator, we have a private moderator's board where we can discuss issues, troublemakers, and so on, to come to agreement on resolutions to those problems.

While this all sounds very time consuming, it needn't be. It only takes a few minutes a day to read and reply to new threads, as well as existing threads that have been busy. The same is true with removing spam and banning troublemakers and competitors who self-promote on your forum. For this reason, many people choose to outsource the operation of their forums, as well as the forum posting itself.

Low-cost outsourcing can remove all of the administrative responsibilities from your day. A friend of mine even has an outsourced assistant log in under his own administrator ID and personally welcome new members to the forums.

Another aspect of outsourcing is paying someone to log in to other forums under your name, and post accordingly. Naturally, this person will need to have enough knowledge to pull it off, but if you can find a reliable assistant—even a virtual assistant overseas—it can be very effective, and it leaves your time free to work on other things, or not to work at all.

Never underestimate the power of forums. Not only will you generate traffic and increase your income, but forums build your good reputation as well.

23

THE HIDDEN VALUE OF CRAIGSLIST AND OTHER INTERNET CLASSIFIEDS SITES

Remember those commercials years ago, claiming that you could easily make thousands of dollars by posting tiny classified ads?

That may have been a scam—in fact, the man behind it went to jail—but you really can make money posting tiny classified ads . . . on the Internet!

I don't know anyone who either advertises in or reads the classified ads in the newspaper anymore. The reason is that classified ads are now free online, they're constantly updated since new ads appear instantly, and there are exponentially more readers online.

The premier classified site is Craigslist and it's the one I prefer.

The beauty of Craigslist is that it's used by a different audience than the people who see your PPC ads, the people reading your articles and press releases, or the people watching your YouTube videos and listening to your iTunes podcasts. It has a different and unique audience from those of all your other promotional tools and strategies, and therefore it can continually expand your own audience and multiply your sales.

The uses for Craigslist are many.

- If you put up a new site, blog, forum, or whatever, you can post an ad announcing it, complete with a live link, on Craigslist. What this does is get you listed in the search engines almost instantly—since Craigslist is an extremely high-traffic site with ever-changing content, Google's crawler, the "Google-bot," crawls and reads Craigslist constantly. It will find your link, follow it, and your new site is immediately added to the Google search engine. This is a far superior alternative to manually submitting your site to Google, which can take up to a whopping six weeks to process.
- Craigslist has a strong local focus, since there are multiple Craigslist sites, each one focusing on a specific city or region. If you're a local salesperson or small business owner, this really benefits you because it's easy to target your local area by posting only on that site, and because more and more people are using Craigslist to find what they want instead of using traditional advertising.
- Since Craigslist is free and because it's so simple to post an ad that appears instantly, it's easy to use Craigslist to test different offers. While I prefer to use AdWords for this, many people starting out don't want to spend money there testing unproven offers and ideas, and therefore Craigslist is a great alternative. It's also a good way to test different ad headlines to determine which ones get you traffic and which don't.
- Craigslist gives you immediate traffic for free. Ads go live almost immediately after posting, and a massive readership sees them. Every time I post there, I can see the spike in traffic to my web site. In addition, because Craigslist is broken down into so many narrow categories, you're getting targeted traffic rather than curious lookers.
- Craigslist has a very noncommercial feel. Because there are no paid advertisements but strictly classifieds, Craigslist retains a

folksy feel that disarms potential new customers and removes the sales resistance that may be triggered by a more commercial site.

Posting on Craigslist is free and easy. Choose your city's Craigslist site, go to the proper category, and click "Post" in the upper right corner.

If you're only selling in your local area, this won't take much effort. Just post your ad every other day—Craigslist has a minimum waiting period for posting the same ad at least 48 hours apart. If you violate this rule too many times, you can get your IP address permanently banned.

Still, you can come up with significantly different ad variations and post them more frequently. Just be careful if the site automatically begins blocking new ads when you try to post them.

If your market is nationwide or even worldwide, like mine, then things begin to get tricky. Craigslist prohibits posting the same ad to multiple cities or countries at the same time, and their system will catch your multiple duplicate ads and block them, and possibly ban your IP address as well.

To get around that problem, you can purchase software that will intelligently work around Craigslist's algorithms and post gradually to different cities. It will also let you enter a multitude of ad headlines as well as ad copy, in order to avoid flagging of duplicates. Disclaimer: Since some of these software packages may violate Craigslist's terms of service, how you use them is up to you and you're on your own if you create any problems for yourself.

Since Craigslist's algorithms change all the time, like most, I'm not going to make specific software recommendations here. You can find current and up-to-date software recommendations at NeverColdCallBook.com.

Large-scale posting is very effective because it not only brings in massive traffic, but adds dozens of backlinks to your site, from one with a very high Google page rank.

Don't overlook free Internet classifieds as a quick and easy way to boost traffic and get new web sites added to search engines instantly.

24

Explode Your List with Free Giveaways

Everyone wants something for free, and everyone is excited to win anything!

Take this recent example: I recently decided to get a Mac Pro computer. I finally got to the point where my iMac—a great computer in its own right—was getting overworked and running slowly due to some of the processor-intensive applications I use, not to mention having Windows XP running side-by-side with Mac's operating system so I could access the rare Windows application I can't get for the Mac.

Then, a friend of mine—a fellow Google AdWords expert—ran an affiliate promotion to sell his AdWords course. Like many affiliate promotions, there were prizes involved, and the top prize was a beautiful new eight-core Mac Pro.

I promoted just to get the Mac Pro.

The commissions weren't even that great. I just wanted the Mac Pro.

Yes, I could've easily afforded to buy one, and I was about to, but there's something about *winning* a product that's far more exciting.

I was thrilled when the big, heavy Mac Pro box arrived. Even though I was at home, I ripped the box open and removed the computer without even taking it first to my office, where it now resides (I'm using it right now to write this book).

I had won the affiliate promotion's top prize.

There's a certain thrill about winning that's unmatched by anything else. In addition, contests like that really bring out the competitive nature in people. When a good marketer runs an affiliate promotion that involves prizes, he'll e-mail standings out to his affiliates every day, complete with teasers like, "Frank is catching up to Joe, will he overtake him? John is just 30 sales short of winning the laptop—will he get it? If Mike pushes a little harder he might win the camera."

You get the idea.

When people receive an e-mail like that, it brings out their competitiveness as well as their desire to win the better prizes, and they'll promote longer and harder, even if it's an unwise move that pulls resources from the affiliate's main business.

In addition, when you see your name below other people's—especially if you're not very far behind—you'll try hard to beat them, if only for bragging rights.

This is especially true with Internet marketers!

So, how can you take advantage of this competitive nature and desire to win that we human beings have?

There are a couple of ways.

You can run an affiliate contest like the one I've just described. Decide on a list of prizes that will be desirable, and that you can afford to give away, with your earnings from the promotion factored in. Don't buy any of the prizes yet because it's easier to have them drop-shipped to your winners, and some people may ask for a cash equivalent, if you're willing to do that.

Announce the prizes up-front and get your affiliates fired up.

Throughout the contest, send out daily e-mails of the day's rankings, complete with comments to bring out everyone's competitive nature.

Then, after all is said and done, order the prizes immediately. I was not only thrilled to win a new Mac Pro, but was even happier at how quickly it arrived.

What if you don't have a large group of good affiliates, or don't even use affiliate marketing?

You can use this strategy too.

In fact, I'm preparing to run a contest with my subscriber list and not my affiliates. I'm putting together a list of prizes—laptop computers, Apple TV, camcorder, Blu-Ray players, and more—and giving my list the ability to participate and win those valuable prizes.

I'm going to do it with my tell-a-friend system (ViralMaxi mizer.com). The person who refers the most people to my site will win first prize, and so on down the list.

Since the winners will be ranked on total number of unique invitations, and not on how many times they use the tell-a-friend tool, people will be encouraged to e-mail to their *entire* address book for *every one* of their e-mail accounts!

This is going to result in ridiculous amounts of new traffic for me.

As a safeguard, there will be minimums for each prize. For example, someone will need to refer at least one thousand people before they'll qualify to win the laptop.

After the contest closes, I'll log in to my back-end, pull up a report of the results, and begin ordering prizes to ship to my winners.

Never forget the competitive nature of humans. If you exploit it properly, you will reap immense rewards.

25

YouTube and Online Video: The New Ultimate Traffic Generator?

Google AdWords may be my top pick for generating highly targeted, high-converting traffic to my sites, but YouTube is running a close second and catching up fast, not to mention the growing number of video sites on the Web.

The reason is simple: More and more people are using YouTube. The technology continues to improve—it now even accepts high-definition video—and it's quickly going mainstream.

Another great thing about YouTube is that Google now owns it, and, since everyone likes to take care of their own, YouTube videos get high rankings in Google search results.

I enjoy using YouTube because it's fairly quick and easy to create a video, especially with today's affordable options, and your message gets across very effectively. I keep my video camera set up and ready to go, so when I have a flash of inspiration I can turn it on and quickly record my thoughts before they go away.

People learn and absorb messages in three different ways: visual, auditory, and by reading. In my videos, I'm able to hit all three. People are watching an image on a screen—me—while also listening to my spoken word, and reading bullet points and other text I add to the video.

The other nice thing about YouTube is all the little tricks you can use to maximize your views, which I'll get to in a minute.

Naturally, you need to begin creating videos. I'm not going to go into technical details here because I covered that in the chapter on vodcasting, and because you can view more detailed information at NeverColdCallBook.com. However, you do need something to talk about, and that's a lot easier than you think.

The way to really fast-track your success with YouTube and get a large number of videos created in a very short time is by accessing your articles. Any good marketer has tons of articles up on the Internet, and if you're new to Internet marketing, it's one of the first things I advise you to do in building your business platform.

Simply turn each of your articles into a video. Read the article through several times to get it into your head, turn on the camera, and start talking. You can't read the article verbatim unless you have a memory like Rain Man; also, it would require an expensive teleprompter and you would probably come across as stiff and formal if you used one.

Instead, get the material into your head, and speak in a conversational tone. Whether you're simply paraphrasing the article or are discussing the subject matter, be upbeat, speak in a firm voice, and of course, dress professionally. I keep a couple of suits and dress shirts in my office so, if I'm dressed casually, I can quickly change, turn on the lights and camera, and begin recording.

The same goes for your vodcasting. Every video I shoot goes both to YouTube and other sites, as well as to my iTunes video podcast. Use the videos everywhere and don't let anything go to waste.

To upload my videos, I don't go directly to YouTube. I use a free tool called TubeMogul.com that, like article-submitting tools, will upload your video to every video site on the net. You register for a free account, go to all of the video sites that TubeMogul submits to, register at all of them, and then enter your log-in information for each site into TubeMogul. Then, every time you upload a new video, you click "Launch" and TubeMogul immediately uploads it to all of those sites. (If you happen to upload a very large volume of videos each month, TubeMogul has paid options to handle that, but even I don't come close to those kinds of numbers, and the free level of membership more than accommodates me.)

This gets you much better exposure, traffic, and views than uploading to YouTube alone, even if it is the premier video site.

Once your videos are online, the next step is to get people viewing them.

People find your videos mostly through searching on YouTube as well as on Google. That's why it's important to use titles and descriptions that are rich in the keywords that bring people to your site. "Sales," "cold calling," "selling," and related terms are frequent in my titles and descriptions. Also, always provide a link to your site in the description; this gives you valuable backlinks on high-ranking sites while providing an easy way for people to click through.

You can also take advantage of current pop culture and current events to maximize your views and traffic. For example, when the movie *The Secret* was the hot topic of conversation, I temporarily changed my video titles to things like, "The Secret to Sales Success" and "The Secret to Never Cold Call Again." Since there were millions upon millions of searches for *The Secret*, and because a disproportionate percentage of those people were small business owners and entrepreneurs, I profited handsomely from using that strategy.

There are some other popular ways to get a high number of views. One is to create a controversial discussion or even an argument in the comments below the video. Someone I know will upload a video and then have all of his friends log in and go to the page under their respective YouTube usernames, and proceed to argue with each other over the video's content. This draws into the argument people who, like forum users, will continue to return over and over again to see what others have posted. This is effective because the more views a video gets, the more prominently it will appear in YouTube's search results.

My favorite way to get big results is to post a new video and then to send an e-mail broadcast to my entire list announcing it. Every time I have done this, the video appeared in the Top 100 videos for that day, and frequently for the next several days as well. Doing this achieves high visibility on YouTube, resulting in endless numbers of people viewing the video, creating a self-perpetuating cycle.

A lifetime total views that's high in number will also help a video to self-perpetuate. I have one video in particular that is my most-viewed of all. To continue growing that number, which keeps the video very prominent on YouTube, I mail it out to my list on a fairly regular basis. This gets thousands of people viewing it in a single day, driving the total number of views even higher and frequently getting the video back into the Top 100.

Another tactic that is unbelievably effective for getting high views, but usually inappropriate, is to use footage or stock photos of bikini models in the center portion of the video, since that's what YouTube's thumbnail image is generated from. As I said, this is inappropriate for most, with exceptions such as those in the fitness and nutrition industries. But teenage boys clicking on your video because of the scantily-clad woman on the thumbnail won't get you any sales, and there's a likelihood that potential customers who might otherwise buy from you could be turned off, so be careful with this one.

Finally, post your videos everywhere. On your blog, forum, social network site, your Facebook and other social networking accounts—everywhere. And mail them to your list. The key to succeeding with this tactic is getting a large number of views in the shortest time possible, launching it to prominence on YouTube so it can self-perpetuate.

26

AFFILIATES: YOUR OWN DEALER/ DISTRIBUTOR NETWORK

During my first several years of marketing online, I didn't even bother looking into affiliate programs. The issue is that I was coming from the mindset of an author.

Before telling that story, what exactly are affiliates?

Affiliates, very simply, are people who refer traffic to your site, and are paid a commission on all sales resulting from that traffic. Or, in rare cases, a small commission for every new visitor they send you. While no one is quite sure who actually invented affiliate marketing, Amazon.com is credited with making it mainstream and is believed to have the largest affiliate network on the world.

This didn't make sense to me because I was in the world of authors. Even before my first published book, *Never Cold Call Again* (John Wiley & Sons, 2006) came out, I was considered a self-published author thanks to the *Cold Calling Is a Waste of Time* home-study course I sell on NeverColdCall.com.

In the world of authors, as a general rule, there are no affiliate programs and affiliate links. Instead, authors trade e-mail promotions with each other. I'll promote someone's book to my list, and in return, he'll promote mine to his list.

It's all a very simple, informal, "I'll scratch your back, you scratch mine" arrangement.

So, thanks to that mindset, I didn't at first understand affiliate marketing. People struck me as greedy when I offered to exchange promotions with them, and they responded with, "Where's my affiliate link?" I was first exposed to this in 2006, when I put together the launch for *Never Cold Call Again*. Other authors were happy to mail with nothing more than the promise of a future promotion from me, but by that time I had begun to connect with people in the Internet marketing world—I had been friends with Tom Beal for a few years, who then introduced me to Mike Filsaime—and was participating in Internet marketing forums and attending a few events.

Every time I asked an Internet marketer whom I'd previously connected with to mail for me, the marketer would ask for an affiliate link. While I initially didn't understand this and suspected it to come from greed, in reality there are a lot of very good reasons why a marketer, myself included, won't send out a promotional mailing without an affiliate link.

For starters, we're all in business to make money. As you'll learn in a future chapter, once you are a prominent marketer with a large following and big list, you can eventually make as much money in affiliate commissions as you do in your main business. This is a really big incentive to avoid sending out mailings for free. Why would I promote someone's book or product for free when I routinely make five figures in commissions by sending out one e-mail?

Next, affiliate mailings dilute one's list. They are a distraction from your main message, and every one will trigger unsubscribes and you'll cut into the size of your list. Therefore, when doing a promotion, a good marketer will make sure the potential commissions are worth a whole lot more than the amount of business he will lose from people who leave his list. As a result of this, I do very few affiliate promotions. They are reserved for products that pay good commissions, that come from reputable people, and that I've personally reviewed before promoting them.

Finally, many affiliate programs pay recurring commissions. If I have to choose between mailing for you and potentially making $5,000, versus mailing for someone else's membership site and making $1,000 per month for the next year, I'll choose the latter. Recurring commissions are always more appealing to a marketer then a single—or no—commission check.

You'll of course need to set up an affiliate program to make this all happen.

A great, all-inclusive system featuring a shopping cart, e-mail, and affiliate program all in one is NeverColdCallCart.com. I've used it extensively, it's inexpensive, and it's fantastic.

Once you're signed up there, you can set up everything you need including your products, affiliate program, and e-mail auto-responder series. It even includes recurring billing and affiliate commissions for membership sites and recurring products.

If you're wondering about commissions, 50 percent is standard in the Internet marketing world; 40 percent if you're selling a physical product, due to the printing/production and other costs.

And, don't forget about contests. They're really the key to taking a good affiliate promotion and making it great.

For more resources on affiliate marketing, including home-study courses that will teach you all the ins and outs of it, see NeverColdCallBook.com.

27

JOINT VENTURES: THE ULTIMATE (AND FASTEST) LIST BUILDERS

Ah, joint ventures. No discussion of Internet marketing would be complete without them. But they can be confusing.

For starters, joint ventures (commonly referred to as JVs) aren't what most people think. In the offline business world, a joint venture typically consists of a formal business agreement that two or more people, or firms, will enter into with specific, clearly defined objectives.

In Internet marketing, however, a JV is any time someone promotes for someone else, or when two people promote for each other. There is no formal written agreement, with the possible exception of an affiliate program.

Confused yet? I was too for a long time. In fact, there is so much gray area and overlap between affiliate marketing and JVs that I wasn't sure if I should even separate them into two different chapters. But, because JVs don't necessarily have to include an affiliate program, and because there are a few things to learn that are specific to JVs, I decided to separate the two.

JVs are, quite simply, the fastest and easiest way to build a large e-mail list.

They're also one of the worst.

Even more confused now? Don't worry, I'll explain.

The common advice to a brand new marketer who has no list is to set up an affiliate program, contact major marketers while sending them a copy of your product, and convince them to promote for you.

The result of this is that, with a well-designed promotion and good e-mail copy, a huge chunk of the big marketer's list will sign up for yours when they visit your web site.

It's not uncommon for a smart and eager newcomer to Internet marketing to offer 75 or even 100 percent commissions to the big gun. This encourages the heavy hitter to really push for you, maybe with several mailings to his list, in order to line his pockets with that full 100 percent commission.

Sure, he knows you're simply out to grab a bunch of his subscribers, but for 100 percent commission, it's worth it.

So now you get some big guns on board to promote for you in return for rich commissions. You put in a lot of time and work, and when it's all over you haven't made any money for yourself, but you've acquired the most basic building block of Internet marketing success—a list of potential buyers—and you've gotten it for free.

That's the good news, and that is the absolute beauty of JVs. Fast and easy list building, frequently to a very large degree. I do stand behind JVs as the first step a total newcomer with no list should take. Create a quality product, get it in the hands of the big gurus, and get them to promote for you at high commissions.

Now let's change the subject completely.

Once people had really gotten to know me in the Internet marketing world, and had come to respect me due to the level of success I'd attained online with NeverColdCall.com, they began asking me to join their affiliate programs and promote their products.

Naturally, I refused most, and today I refuse nearly all offers since I have a core group I'm willing to promote for, but only for people with stellar reputations whom I came to know and trust, like Mike Filsaime and Russell Brunson. After all, my list consists almost exclusively of salespeople. I know sales appealed to me personally as a career because I am enterprising and desire a high income, so surely they'd respond to offers for Internet marketing courses. The balance of my list consists of entrepreneurs, so promoting these offers to them was a no-brainer.

I did a few promotions and something bizarre happened: I consistently came in at or near the top of most promotions and contests I'd participated in.

Last year, I mailed a promotion and came in at #1 for affiliates who didn't bribe their lists to buy (I was #3 overall; the #1 and #2 affiliates gave away freebies at their own expense to entice people to buy the JV offer.)

This not only blew me away, but shocked all the big-name marketers whom I'd beaten out; after all, most had lists of 400,000, 500,000 or even more, while my rather modest list of about 100,000 had generated double or triple the amount of sales.

It was a shock at first, but it quickly made sense once I'd analyzed the situation.

You see, because I don't sell products within the Internet marketing niche, my list consists exclusively of salespeople, small business owners, and other entrepreneurs. It was built by directing highly targeted traffic to my site, mostly through AdWords but through many other methods as well. It was not built with JVs.

By contrast, most of these big guns were actively doing JVs, and their lists were built almost exclusively through JVs.

The result?

They all have the same names on their respective lists.

When you have a bunch of people who constantly do JVs with each other within the same niche, what eventually happens is that anyone who subscribes to one marketer's newsletter eventually subscribes to them all. The end result is that a marketer who had a massive list of, say, 300,000 people, may only wind up with 10,000 exclusives, or even fewer.

Compare that with my list, which, although much smaller, is almost 100 percent exclusive.

The exclusivity of my list gives me the power to blow out gurus with massively larger lists.

And, it hurts them in promotions because by the time someone receives their e-mail, odds are high that they've already bought through another marketer's affiliate link.

This is also the cause of the phenomenon of receiving a dozen e-mails, all at the same time—the precise launch time—for the same product. They're all trying to be first with their affiliate link in order to shut out competing marketers.

Then, I mosey along two or three days later, drop an e-mail to my exclusive list, and instantly become one of the top affiliates in the promotion.

So, in conclusion, while JVs really are the fastest and easiest way to build a large list—and I highly recommend them—they're not the best way to build a strong, exclusive list. Don't get lazy after a successful JV or two. Instead, consider that your foundation to get you started, and move on to all the other traffic generation methods explained in this book and elsewhere.

Check out NeverColdCallBook.com to see real results from various JVs I've participated in.

28

Triple Your Results (or More) with Viral Tell-A-Friend Systems

I've made it no secret that I am a huge, raving fan of using tell-a-friend mechanisms. They are a simple yet highly effective way of spreading the word about your site.

Viral marketing is key to most huge online success stories.

By the way, it's not called viral because it will make you sick. It's called viral because it spreads as fast as a virus—just as quickly and to just as many people.

Hotmail, for example, exploded because of the little "get your free Hotmail account here" link that was automatically inserted into every e-mail message. Because free e-mail accounts were practically unheard of back in 1996, people went wild over that link. It spread so rapidly that Microsoft purchased Hotmail for a reported $400 million just a year later, leaving Hotmail's creators exceedingly wealthy and set for life.

Twitter is another great example. When I began using Twitter last year, I had no idea it had been in existence for well over a year already. It didn't take long to become a household name from that point forward. Twitter had finally gained enough users to reach that proverbial tipping point where something that had a built-in viral mechanism explodes and achieves prominence.

Now, bear with me here as I explain the science behind why viral marketing is so effective. It may sound confusing at first but it's really quite simple.

The *viral exponent* is a metric used to track the growth of your site. A viral exponent of 1.0 means that your site gets the same number of visitors every day on autopilot (no external factors like AdWords or other traffic generators are included). In other words, if 100 people visit your site today, 100 new ones will come tomorrow, and each day thereafter.

Now, don't get too excited here. A viral exponent of 1.0 is difficult to achieve. Even rarer is anything above 1.0, say, 1.01. That is in the realm of Twitter and Hotmail. If you can figure out how to get a site to a viral exponent of 1.01, you will be the next Internet billionaire, and if that's the case, please call me immediately so I can invest in your new venture.

I'll be the first to admit that I have not yet achieved a viral exponent of 1.0 with NeverColdCall.com. As I said, it's hard to do. But you will need to get close to 1.0 in order for your business to prosper and for you to become wealthy. There's no way around it.

As I write this, the American economy is in the middle of a severe recession and credit crunch. Businesses are closing left and right, bankruptcies are rampant, as are foreclosures and job losses.

Despite all that, my businesses are at an all-time high. Sales are nearly *triple* what they were just a few years ago, around 2006.

The reason? It has nothing to do with the economy, good or bad. It has everything to do with viral marketing, and getting my viral exponent as high as I possibly can.

Heck, if I'd figured this stuff out back in 2006 at the height of the economic boom, I'd probably be ultrawealthy and permanently retired from business by now.

The key to my success in spite of a difficult economy is continually growing my business through viral marketing. Many things I've already taught you will accomplish this even though you don't realize it on the surface.

YouTube is a powerful viral mechanism. People who watch and like your videos will forward them to your friends. The same goes with news articles—remember that "send to a friend" link in Yahoo! News?

Podcasts, vodcasts, and much more all fall into this category. They not only bring you new traffic, but they also give people easy ways to tell their friends about you. What can be easier than forwarding a video or article?

29

USE ONLINE CONTESTS TO GENERATE MASSIVE TRAFFIC SPIKES

Everyone who is working or has worked in sales knows the effectiveness of sales contests. The company will offer prizes such as a big screen TV to the first-place winner, a new laptop for second-place, an iPod for third-place, and so on.

Why aren't you taking advantage of contests in *your* business?

If you have a sales staff, you can easily implement what I've just described. If you already have done this, then congratulations! However, sales contests are just the beginning.

If you are an entrepreneur or Internet marketer who doesn't have a sales staff, please read on as well.

The effective results of contests are many.

- Contests entice people to produce with a variety of enticing prizes.

- Contests bring out the instinctive competitive nature of human beings, causing them to produce high results in order to beat out everyone else involved.
- Contests get people—existing and prospective customers— excited and hyped up to participate and do business with you.
- Contests are an amazing way to really increase the size of your list in a short period of time.

Following are some examples of creative uses of contests that are certainly outside the box and extremely effective.

A contest can be used to motivate people to send you referrals and new customers. One example of how to accomplish that is by creating a contest offering prizes to your existing customers and/or subscribers via a tell-a-friend mechanism. Send a couple of advance notices to your lists notifying them that the contest is coming up. Be sure to list all of the great prizes, and send them to a page listing them again and displaying photos of those prizes. Set a time limit for the contest—perhaps Monday through Sunday—and be sure to use a system like ViralMaximizer.com so you can easily track who is sending referrals, and how many, in order to award prizes accurately.

Another contest idea is, when launching a new product, award "first mover" bonuses to the first several customers. For example, the first five people to buy might get a free one-hour consulting call with you. The next 20 might get a group coaching call with you. The next 50 may receive an inexpensive but valuable prize like an iPod Shuffle. The next 100 may receive an autographed copy of a book or product of yours, the next 500 may get a free digital download package, and so on, as far as you want to take it.

As each first mover bonus sells out, immediately e-mail your list to let them know it's gone, and that they'd better move quickly before the rest are sold out.

A relaunch of an existing product with lagging sales can be done in the same way. Announce that you're doing a one-week special promotion that will include many fabulous free prizes to people who buy within that time period. You may even want to award the same prize to every person who buys during that time. This is very effective for reigniting a good product that has stagnant sales, and helps to create buzz and push sales for quite a while after the contest ends.

A word of warning: When running a contest to promote an existing product, it's a good idea to exclude existing customers from receiving the e-mails. I failed to do so once—and only once—and was barraged by angry customers, screaming that they already own the product and therefore should get freebies too! Even people who had bought a year ago or longer were demanding prizes. So, keep that in mind, since forgetting it will waste a lot of your time and really damage your attitude for a while as well.

I've already covered affiliate contests in a previous chapter so I won't cover that again here, except to remind you that there are lots of variations you can use. You can award physical prizes, time for coaching and/or consulting with you, or even cash.

Also, many effective marketers will run affiliate contests not for sales, but for total opt-ins. (As I mentioned in Chapter 24, I won the Mac Pro computer I'm using right now as a result of sending another marketer 1,500 opt-ins during his contest.) In this case, you set the minimum number of opt-ins an affiliate must get you for each particular prize. Or, in the case of my Mac Pro, the computer was given away for everyone who sent in at least 1,500 opt-ins.

Get creative with prizes. I'm sure there are plenty more great ideas I haven't even thought of yet. I'd love to see you beat me to it!

For sample pages, contest ideas, and more, check out NeverColdCallBook.com.

30

CREATE MASSIVE PROFITS IN MINIMAL TIME WITH PRODUCT LAUNCHES

Most people new to Internet marketing believe that you can create or purchase a product, build a web site, put it online, and the product will sell.

Wrong.

Other people think you can put a product and web site online, follow many of the techniques suggested in this book—such as Google AdWords, blogging, and other methods—and your product will sell.

This is true and it works very effectively. In fact, that's how I started out. I quit my job and in less than six weeks I was making an income of $6,000 per month, using only Google AdWords and a few basic e-mail and copywriting ideas. However, I wasn't an instant millionaire, as many people picture an Internet marketer. My income did grow and it wasn't long before it became quite substantial, but still, it was gradual. It took a few years before I could fully enjoy the millionaire lifestyle.

However, there is a way to get there a lot faster, and that's with a well-orchestrated product launch, followed by additional launches as you introduce new products.

What is a product launch? Quite simply, it's a gradual series of events that build anticipation, curiosity, and desire for your new product.

It's one thing to create a new product and announce it to your list. It will probably sell, but few people will be very excited about it, and there won't be an explosion of buzz all over the Internet about it.

However, when you slowly and gradually create anticipation, and only release the product when people can't stand it anymore and just have to have it, not only can you potentially make millions of dollars in a very short time—I know someone who pulled off a perfect launch and sold out in just a few hours, to the tune of three million dollars—but your product will endure for the long haul.

Look at books, for example. When I launched my first book, *Never Cold Call Again*, I did it with a huge launch. Not only did the book become an instant bestseller, hitting #1 on Amazon within three hours, and making the *New York Times* business best-seller list for that month, but it also continues to sell extremely well today with absolutely no promotion from me. Seriously—I do nothing to promote that book anymore. It's a consistent and long-term top-selling sales book on Amazon and everywhere else.

Here are the basic steps to pulling off an effective launch. Credit goes to Jeff Walker, from whom I learned much of this. You can find links to his sites and products at NeverColdCallBook.com.

First, you need to set up a separate e-mail list that is dedicated to the product launch. Then, send an e-mail out to your full list, announcing something to the effect of, "I've got something new and *really* exciting coming soon, but because so many competitors would love to steal it and get it to you first, I can't talk about it just yet. Yes, it's *that* good. If you would like to receive periodic updates on the new product and when it will be available, please sign up at this page."

An alternate strategy is to think of the biggest problem that your new product or service solves, and send an e-mail describing it and saying, "To get the solution to this [or these] challenges, sign up here."

The reason for this is so that you don't pummel your list with too many e-mails, resulting in mass unsubscribe requests. Besides, your core customers and biggest fans—the ones who are going to buy the product anyway—will surely sign up right away so you won't have to worry about missing them. I would suggest, however, that you use e-mail software that can track who has and who hasn't opened the e-mail, so you can send it again later only to people who never read it before. I'll give you specific software and service providers in an upcoming chapter.

Once you're got your launch list ready to go, the prelaunch phase starts. My preference here is to avoid discussing the product just yet, and instead to send out a series of communications that discuss problems, along with their solutions. The most powerful way to go about this is to discuss a problem or challenge, touch on a solution, then mention another—and bigger—problem your subscribers may have, or talk about something they probably want. Then, close your message by telling them, "I'll give you the answer to that next week, so stay tuned."

This is what Jeff calls the "soap opera effect." Soap operas and other drama series keep people hooked by always ending each episode with some kind of cliffhanger—something they'll be dying to know, but will have to tune in next week to learn about. You will do the same. Your subscribers will be drooling for your next communication.

The forms of the specific messages should be varied. Different people prefer different formats, so you should include e-mail (obviously), blog posts, videos, and maybe even brief podcasts.

You might send one message as a plain-text e-mail. The next might come as a link to a blog post.

A great way to increase your blog traffic and get people subscribing to your blog's feed is to send an e-mail that generates excitement, then immediately has a "Click here to continue reading" link.

Putting a video on YouTube and sending out a teaser e-mail with a link to it works very well. You might even want to send one out to your full list just once, since it will create a nice traffic spike for that video, resulting in new subscribers who will jump on the bandwagon.

How you wrap up the prelaunch and move on to the actual launch day can vary. Many marketers, particularly well-known ones, like to announce the actual product itself and tell people, "It's coming Monday at 12 noon Eastern," or whatever your launch time might be.

What I prefer is to keep the teasing up until the actual launch. In other words, people are extremely excited but have no idea of what I'm going to offer them. I close the prelaunch series with something like, "I've discussed a lot of problems over the past few weeks, and have given you lots of solutions. But that's only a tiny part of the story. Mark your calendars and be at your computers next Tuesday at 12 noon Eastern, because that's when I'm making the big announcement to the world. You're finally going to get ALL the answers on that date and time, and only for a short time, so don't miss it!"

Naturally, I send an "It's Live!" e-mail at the precise launch day and time.

That's a brief explanation of product launches, and it's enough to get you started with an effective one of your own. Combine that with a product launch contest (first mover bonuses), a strong affiliate contest, and maybe even a tell-a-friend contest for your subscribers to get more people on board, and hold on to your seat when launch day comes.

And talk with your web hosting provider to make sure they're prepared. Servers and data centers routinely crash during great launches.

For more specifics on product launches and where you can get a lot more information, see NeverColdCallBook.com.

Part V

TURNING TRAFFIC
INTO SALES

31

HOME PAGE STRUCTURE: MORE IMPORTANT THAN YOU THINK

There's a lot of talk about copywriting, and rightly so. Your web site copy—the actual text and graphics on the pages—is so important that marketers who have the money routinely pay $25,000 or more to a top copywriter, just for *one page*!

(Don't worry, you won't have to spend that kind of money on copy. I never have nor do I ever plan to.)

While copy is important—so important that I've dedicated a chapter to it—it's sort of like putting the cart before the horse. Before you can write good copy, you have to create an effective web site structure that maximizes your return on your marketing efforts.

Structure is a largely ignored part of Internet marketing— everyone seems to be hung up on generating more traffic and writing copy—yet it's so powerful that testing and incorporating various elements of structure to my sites has done more to increase my sales than everything else *combined*.

Part of structure includes web site conversion mechanisms, not just the layout of the site. In fact, just a few of my secret mechanisms are responsible for more than tripling my sales volume—instantly!

I'm sorry to say that I'm not going to reveal my best secrets to you here. To be frank (no pun intended), that knowledge is simply too valuable to me. I developed it over years and years of endless testing, and it's so effective that I cannot run the risk of letting competitors gain access to it. Nor do I want another marketer laying claim to inventing it.

Even the biggest and most well-known Internet marketing gurus in the world haven't figured them out; however, if I do decide to reveal them someday, probably when I retire completely (which in all honestly will be relatively soon), I'll announce it to my newsletter, so go sign up at NeverColdCallBook.com.

One last note before moving on: As important as copywriting is for your sales page, you need to get people there in the first place! What good is great copy if nobody ever sees it? Poor web site structure will prevent people from ever seeing your sales page (this problem is otherwise known as a filter in the marketing world, since filters keep things—or people—out).

The first part of structure is your home page (or landing page).

Your singular goal on this page, as you know by now, is to get an opt-in. An e-mail sign-up. That's it!

However, most Internet marketers do a notoriously bad job of accomplishing this. Let's start with an example—have you ever seen a home page like the one in Figure 31.1? (And I know you have.)

A lot of marketers wrongly believe this to be effective, because it gives the visitor absolutely no other option but to enter their name and e-mail address in order to even gain access to the site. This is known as a *straight* (or *pure*) "squeeze page." If you notice, not only does it lack information but it contains no menu bar either.

In theory, this seems like a good idea. If people are forced to sign up just to view the site, they're going to sign up, right?

Wrong! Straight squeeze pages suck.

"Learn the secrets to Never Cold Calling Again..."

INSIDE: How I became a top sales rep with no leads, no cold calling, no prospecting, and how you can too. Learn how to get a steady supply of hot leads calling you, ready and willing to <u>buy</u>!

Get instant access now:

* First Name:

* Your Email Address:

Submit

Figure 31.1

While many marketers mistakenly believe that it's a good idea to give a visitor only one option, the fact of the matter is that they always have at least *two* options—the second being to leave your site without signing up.

Most people will instantly click the back button on their browser, sending your bounce rate through the roof (bounce rate is the percentage of people who immediately leave your site). It's one thing to use a squeeze page that has good copy and lots of credibility generators, but a nearly empty page like this that provides almost zero clue as to what you're selling, and no proof of your credibility, will kill your business.

Now, it's one thing if you're extremely well-known. Anthony Robbins can get away with this because everyone knows who he is, and he has serious credibility. Jeffrey Gitomer and I could probably get away with it on a site that is targeted solely toward salespeople, because we're two of the biggest names in that niche.

If you don't yet have that level of prominence, avoid a straight squeeze page.

Here's why.

First of all, I've already mentioned the sky-high bounce rate this is going to cause unless you're already a celebrity or rock star. That's going to kill your opt-in rate and your sales volume.

Another issue is that it gives people absolutely no clue as to who you are or what you're selling. With so many viruses and worms all over the Internet, not to mention identity theft and phishing, people are simply way too guarded about typing their information into a mysterious site with no identity.

But here is the big killer: I've signed up for a few of these sites, and they had great products that I wanted to buy. However, when I went back to the site to purchase, I was slapped in the face with that stupid squeeze page. I'd have to enter my name and e-mail address each and every time I wanted to visit, and that is unacceptable.

Talk about a major filter! Guess what happened when I went back to purchase? That's right—I got annoyed and clicked my back button, sending the site's bounce rate even higher, and costing them a sale as well as future business.

Many so-called marketing gurus are still advocating the straight squeeze page, but I know both from my own experiences as a potential customer, as well as from heavy testing on my own sites, that they simply don't work, unless of course you're already a household name in your niche.

The next level up is from a straight squeeze page is one that does contain information, credibility boosters, and even testimonials, but has no menu. Since it's too big to include here, please go to your computer and pull up the following page before continuing (if you don't have access to a computer right now, bookmark or dog-ear this page and come back to it, because it's far too important to miss):

NeverColdCallBook.com/oldhome

This one does work a lot better in getting opt-ins. I've tested it thoroughly, and bounce rate is a lot lower, and opt-in rate is a lot higher.

However, there still a big problem here, and that's the filter effect—the major sales killer.

Again, if I return to the site wanting to buy the product, I'm forced once again to enter my name and e-mail address. My testing showed that while this page corrects the opt-in problem—almost, but not completely—it still destroys sales. That's because most people don't buy on the first visit. They buy later on, after thinking about the purchase, or getting a few of my follow-up e-mails.

However, when they go back to the site, there's that squeeze page again!

And, contrary to popular belief, a significant number of subscribers don't read entire follow-up e-mails and click the link at the very end. Instead, they'll go and type in your site's URL halfway through, or simply come back another time altogether. You'd be surprised at how many.

So, what's the answer? This page is the result of over six years of intensive, never-ending tests. Again, please pull this page up on your computer for review: NeverColdCallBook.com/newhome.

What's different? Well, the biggest change is that there's a full sidebar on the page, including a menu.

Some people will tell you that a menu is a bad thing, because a few people will scroll around the site without bothering to sign up, and will subsequently leave.

I'm here to tell you that's a good thing, because in comparing large lists of subscribers versus customer lists for the same time period, it turns out that about a quarter of all customers *never subscribed to my list!*

That's right—one-fourth of my site's visitors didn't care to join my list. They went straight to the sales page, and bought.

When I was using a straight squeeze page, or even one containing everything here except for the menu bar, I was losing them all by putting up the squeeze page filter. Dropping the stupid squeeze resulted in a 33 percent increase in sales—*instantly!*

What could you do with an immediate 33 percent sales boost? Because if you use a squeeze page with no navigation, that's exactly what you're leaving on the table. If you're making $5,000 a month right now, you can give yourself an instant raise to over $6,600 a month by dropping that silly squeeze.

Moving on, your next goal is, of course, to get that sign-up.

Before we do that, I need to give you a legal notice: My own page is just for the sake of example. You are not authorized in any way, shape, or form, to copy or otherwise use it. It is copyrighted. If you do try to copy or steal it, I can assure you that my copyright attorney is one of the best in the country, and you'll be hearing from him.

Ok, with the dirty business out of the way, let's continue analyzing the page.

Looking at the previous example—the current page I use today—you can see that I start off with an attention-getting headline, followed by a subhead that tells them what they're getting for free.

A video is beneath that, followed by a brief video from me explaining what the free download contains.

Next comes an official-looking highlighted "Download Instructions" followed by another pitch to sign up. This one makes it clear that they're subscribing for a newsletter and not just a free download, which is very important to prevent spam complaints that might get you into trouble with your web host, or even fined or, worst case, getting your hosting account shut down entirely.

Then there is that all-important sign-up form, along with a photo of yours truly.

My photo is captioned with some real credibility builders; figure out which ones you can use that are true and verifiable, and use them.

Below that comes more information about what the site is all about, followed by a testimonial that includes a photo—these are a lot more believable since so many marketers write fake ones—plus a few bullet-points as to what visitors will get in return for subscribing, and another opt-in form.

I have found that two opt-in forms, one at the very beginning of the page immediately following the offer, along with a second one following additional reasons to sign up, works best.

At the very bottom of the page are additional testimonials from two people who are prominent in my target niche. If you're a regular, offline small business, then use strong testimonials from happy customers here along with the photo testimonial.

Video testimonials work great too if you can get one.

In the left sidebar you see a menu, followed by a brief bio of myself, media credentials, and another box below containing links to learn more about my speaking and coaching services.

In all honestly, the site sells few speaking or coaching gigs—there are better ways to get those—but the very fact that I do paid speaking and coaching is a huge credibility booster.

Even if you've never done paid speaking or coaching, it can't hurt to at least put the offer up. It will increase your sign-ups and conversions, and every now and then you'll actually get a paid speaking gig as a result.

Once someone signs up, they are redirected to my tell-a-friend page, and are then redirected to my sales page. I won't go into sales page structure here because there are no hard and fast rules you need to follow there, other than keeping the header and sidebars consistent throughout your entire site. The sales page is all about copy, and that comes next.

You'll notice that I talk about testing and split-testing quite a bit in this book. I never stop testing new ideas, no matter how crazy and farfetched they may seem at first, because every now and then, one of them works. As a result, what you actually see on my live web sites may sometimes vary from what I'm including in this book. Don't let that scare you—it's probably just another test, and if I discover something that works better than what I've described here, you'll be notified at NeverColdCallBook.com.

For more great tips, split-test results, and additional examples of effective landing page structure, visit NeverColdCallBook.com.

32

WRITING COPY: YOUR ONLINE SALES PRESENTATION

I mentioned earlier that many marketers *mistakenly* believe that copywriting is the most important element of Internet marketing.

I place emphasis on the word mistakenly because it's only a mistake if your focus is solely on the copy.

You see, just like your business, your copy isn't going to work unless it's standing on a solid, strong foundation.

Your web site structure is that foundation. Once the home page is built properly, is getting a high opt-in rate and a low bounce rate, and redirects new subscribers to a tell-a-friend page before sending them to the sales page, you have that solid foundation and can begin making it pay off.

You do that with great copy.

First of all, I'd like to give credit where credit is due. I first began learning copywriting in earnest from Dr. Joe Vitale through his fantastic books and products (in fact, once we'd become friends, he helped me tweak my sales pages).

Next, I read Joe Sugarman's books. Joe is perhaps the most successful direct marketer in the world—he's the genius behind the BluBlocker sunglasses you've undoubtedly seen on television and in stores.

Then I discovered Michael Fortin and began to read his blog and follow him on Twitter regularly.

There are countless other copywriters and marketers I've studied and learned from, and I've eventually tried—after thoroughly testing and measuring—as many of their ideas as possible.

Those years of testing that have resulted in the copy I use today.

As I'm writing this, I pulled up the software that tracks, tests, and measures all of my sales results.

As of today, my conversion rate for *first-time* visitors—not all visitors—is a whopping 6.3 percent!

By first-time visitors only, I mean people who have never visited the site before and are not on my list.

Granted, there are other factors involved, such as running heavily optimized AdWords campaigns, and employing viral marketing. Still, that's a conversion rate that's almost unheard-of and never even reached by most gurus, save for promotions to their own list. Keep in mind that most of these people have never heard of me before they land on my site.

My sales page contains many elements that will be required for any great sales page. They are:

- A headline, or, in my case, two headlines.
- Subheadlines (or subheads) throughout the page.
- Occasional graphics and product images.
- Testimonials and credibility builders.
- The copy itself, which includes the product description and bonuses.

As to structure, sales pages are open to suggestions. There is no hard-and-fast rule other than including the same header and sidebar elements as are in all other pages for consistency.

I'll take you through my sales page at NeverColdCall.com as an example—it's the "Our System" link in the menu. I find that it's easier to learn by example, even easier than through a book or seminar. Again, a legal warning: You must not copy or otherwise steal my page. If you do, my attorney will be after you!

Once you arrive at the page, you'll see two big, bold headlines on top. One is posed as a question—test results show that putting phrases or questions in quotation marks generates more sales—and the other is a hypnotic phrase, telling the readers to imagine themselves in a certain situation. It may come as no surprise that what they're imagining is what my product promises to do!

Joe Vitale calls this "hypnotic marketing." You put the reader into a state of already imagining and feeling like they've achieved exactly the result they had hoped to find by visiting your site.

The goal, as Joe explains, is to put the reader into a waking trance. If you don't know what a waking trance is, have you ever been driving to a destination other than home, but mistakenly took your home exit without even thinking about it?

That's a waking trance. Your mind is running on autopilot, and you're not consciously directing the action.

Yes, it is a form of hypnosis.

That's our goal with sales copy—to get people to picture themselves living out their desires. It puts the mind on autopilot and sends sales through the roof.

Below that, there's an introduction and the sales letter begins.

As you can see by reading it, it's written in a very personal style, as though I'm writing a letter to an old friend. That's why it's really called a "sales *letter*" and not just "sales page." It's where all the action happens—where you speak personally to the visitor to get him or her to take action.

Note that the sales letter contains plenty of hypnotic elements, such as the line beginning with, "Think of how your life might change...."

This is powerful stuff.

You'll notice a subhead that gives a friendly challenge to the visitor. Challenges like this act as teasers. They are bold yet playful, and further draw the reader into the letter, curious to find out what comes next.

Then comes the personal introduction. Hey, I have to do it sooner or later, so it might as well be immediately after I may have come across as a jerk or otherwise pissed off a reader. The intro adds a more personal touch, and positions me as a great guy who is here to help.

Following that, I explain how the product came to be, and why. I boast that it's really, really good. It works.

I further disarm the reader by stating, "Do I have something to sell you? Of course I do."

This adds a further level of honesty and trust. I immediately follow that with two strong testimonials, providing proof that my product does work and people are happy with it.

Then I switch gears again to a hypnotic statement. I explain that sure, people who use my system get a lot more sales, and they also work a lot less than their colleagues. They have more free time to spend with family and enjoying hobbies.

This is powerful because I'm no longer selling a "how to make more money" product. I'm selling a "how to better enjoy your life" product, and that's what people *really* want.

Why sell the means to an end instead of just addressing the end goal in itself?

Then there's the product image, followed by a very strong endorsement from a powerful influencer.

Then there's the core of it all: the offer. The product itself, what's included, the price, and the terms.

Immediately following the offer comes more verification of proof with a seal provided by a third-party watchdog group verifying that I honor my free trials and money-back guarantees 100 percent of the time, no questions asked.

This seal alone gave me a 36 percent increase in sales!

Thirty-six percent!

The power of third-party certification is limitless.

After that comes my personal favorite part of the sales letter, what I call the curiosity bullet points.

I'm not sure if marketers have a formal name for the curiosity bullet-points, but they've been around practically forever. I remember seeing them in catalogs and magazine ads as a little kid.

They've been around forever because they work.

Adding them to the page provided a more than 50 percent increase in sales.

Unreal? No. They're *that* powerful.

The bullet points give tons of hints as to what's included in the product, or what it can do, without actually revealing those things. It makes people so crazy with curiosity that they simply can't stand it anymore and they order your product just to find out.

Interestingly, I noticed that not only did sales explode when I added the curiosity bullet points, but, for some reason, the refund rate dropped noticeably. I neither know nor understand the reasons behind this, except that people may be sold much more thoroughly by the bullet points and therefore will put more work into getting maximum results from the product.

You'll notice that one of my final bullet points reads,

"A psychological trick to get people to BUY RIGHT NOW . . ."

This is a bit of neurolinguistic programming, otherwise known as NLP.

The phrase "BUY RIGHT NOW" is an embedded command that bypasses the conscious mind and goes straight to the subconscious, where the brain receives and processes it, and sends a command to the conscious mind telling the reader to, you guessed it, BUY RIGHT NOW!

A word of warning, however: You need to be very careful with embedded commands. If the reader picks up on it and can see what you're doing, it's not going to work. I can get away with that one because "buy right now" is exactly what salespeople want their prospects to do. It's what they're paid for, after all, so they don't interpret the phrase as an embedded command. They interpret it as a desirable outcome of buying my product.

Immediately following the bullet points, and especially the "buy right now" command, is a link to purchase. At this point in the sales letter, the reader is drooling at the mouth to buy, so that's where I let them take the bait.

Below that are more details and deeper descriptions of what they get when they buy. Much like my home page, this is designed to completely convince someone who wasn't at that point yet when they arrived at the first purchase link.

Another link follows that section.

Further still comes a long list of free bonuses that are immediately downloadable when someone buys. This adds tremendous value—the product itself is $97 at the time of this writing, while the bonuses add up to $300 ($300 is a realistic number relative to the product price and to the fact that the bonuses are instantly accessible—a ridiculous number like $5,000 in bonuses is unrealistic and will make you look like a snake-oil salesman).

Beneath the bonuses you'll find more product details, more hypnotic statements about the better life the product will provide, more details on the risk-free guarantee, all with multiple purchase links spread throughout.

Why is the page so seemingly complex and somewhat long, but not pages long?

It's because there are three kinds of people who will land on the site.

- Readers. These people will read the entire letter from start to finish, unless of course they click on one of the purchase links before reaching the end.
- Skimmers. These people tend to jump from one subhead to the next, skimming the material in between before jumping again. They are the reason why subheads are important.
- Buyers. They are already presold and jump right to an order link. They're the reason I have an "Order Now" button right in my menu structure.

As I close this chapter, I want to remind you that it's only the beginning, only a starting point. You will get amazing results just from using the advice given here, which includes a few of those secret gems that no one else is using. Copywriting, however, is a lifetime study and I strongly encourage you to learn as much as you can about it, and never stop learning.

For links to top copywriters' web sites, home study courses, books, and more, see NeverColdCallBook.com.

33

Your E-Mail Follow-Up System: Long-Term Profits on Autopilot

In the world of seasoned Internet marketers, or even beginners who have gained at least a basic working knowledge of marketing online, an e-mail follow-up system is a total no-brainer. They know it's a basic building block of any successful Internet business, and you can't prosper—or even survive—without one.

Among existing small business owners and entrepreneurs, however—and that's for whom this book is especially written—a surprising majority don't understand the power and necessity of e-mail follow-up, and don't even have lead capture forms on their landing pages.

The problem is so great that dozens of people are earning six-figure incomes simply working with local small businesses to add a lead-generation form and e-mail follow-up series to their web sites (if you want to learn how to do that for a living yourself—it's really easy money for very simple work—visit NeverColdCallBook.com).

Here's the bottom line: Only about 40 percent of first-time visitors to my site will buy the product. The other 60 percent are people who have signed up for my newsletter, and after a few or many follow-up e-mails, they are finally convinced or the need has arisen, and they come back and buy.

Without the e-mail follow-up series, all of those 60 percent would be lost. A site that earns $5,000 per month would drop to $2,000. Ten thousand dollars would drop to $4,000. You get the idea.

In many cases, such as in a product launch, the e-mail follow-ups themselves are the actual core of the marketing system, and not just a way to boost sales that may already be coming in.

Basic e-mail follow-up is simple: Someone signs up at your opt-in form, and then they receive a series of prewritten, pretimed e-mails.

I have about a year's worth of prewritten e-mails in my auto-responder series. I do write new ones from time to time, and add them to the end of my series, but I find that a year is more than enough, especially considering the fact that I send out frequent real-time broadcast messages to my entire list, so they're still going to get content from me whether or not they've reached the end of the series.

Interestingly, I find that people who take any longer than a few months to buy have a much higher refund and chargeback rate than those who buy sooner. This is presumably because they were never fully sold on the product, and therefore never truly believed that it would help them. Because of this, I've thought about limiting the length of my autoresponder series, but I believe this would disappoint many of my good customers who continue to enjoy the e-mails after they've already bought, and because the people who buy after several months and keep the product still greatly outnumber the ones who return it.

I have two main formats for my follow-up e-mails. One is a straight newsletter type of e-mail. I'll choose a topic that's of interest to my audience and write about it, typically a problem and solution e-mail. At the very end I include a brief sales pitch to buy my product—a soft-sell, since the reader is already partly sold by having joined my list in the first place, and because I've just given them some really helpful information that qualifies me as an expert.

The other main format I use is a question-and-answer e-mail. I take actual e-mails that readers send in and respond with my answer or solution. I also post testimonials in my Q&A e-mails in order to further sell the reader on why they should buy my product—hearing about other people's successes with it is very effective. I respond to the testimonial e-mails with a brief congratulations and a thank-you to the person for actually putting my product to work, rather than failing to implement it as many customers unfortunately do.

To make the most of my autoresponder series, I have a lot more than just plain e-mail content. I vary the content quite a bit—such as sending out YouTube videos as well as iTunes podcasts. I'll sometimes use the "Click here to read more" trick to increase traffic to a particular site or blog. I use various multimedia platforms and include them in my autoresponder series (see NeverColdCallBook.com for an up-to-date list of specifics), which hit the subscriber from various angles—reading, listening, and watching (video).

As to the technical details, here are a few.

On the HTML versus text debate, I now send all of my e-mails in HTML. The reason is that you can track open rates on HTML e-mails. In other words, you can see how many people have opened the e-mail and how many haven't. This is very powerful in testing different subject lines to determine which variations get the most opens.

Even more powerful, you can resend the e-mail only to the people who never opened the first one. This is so effective because you can get it in front of them again without annoying the people who did open it, which would result in lots of unsubscribes.

With HTML e-mails, you can also track all of the links in an e-mail and have them appear as normal hyperlinks, rather than a long and ugly tracking link with a dozen random characters at the end. And yes, you can track who has and has not clicked on specific links in e-mails, and handle them accordingly,

The other big debate in e-mail marketing is single versus double opt-in.

Single opt-in means that someone simply signs up for your newsletter and they become subscribed and active.

With double opt-in, a new subscriber must first click on a verification link that your system sends out before they become an active subscriber and begin receiving your e-mails.

The consensus seems to believe that double opt-in is better, but I disagree.

(As with all things in marketing, test both methods on your site and find out what works best for you. My money is on single opt-in!)

I had always used single opt-in, until my e-mail service provider notified me that, due to the large size of my list, they had forced me into double opt-in.

This was back in 2006, and it worked fine for a long time. There was no measurable loss in sales.

Then, about a year ago, I noticed that sales had begun to get sluggish, and things were slowing down with no drop in traffic; in fact, traffic was up. I immediately went to work trying to figure out what was happening. Was it the economy, or was it my marketing?

Needless to say, I tried a countless number of things, measuring them all (this intensive improvement process resulted in many of the ideas presented in this book). One of those things was to set up my own mail server and host my own list.

The results blew my mind.

First of all, my mail deliverability went way up. This simply means how many people are actually receiving my e-mails, versus how many are being blocked by spam filters.

With my own server, the e-mails being sent are mine and only mine, and I'm careful to write content that won't trigger spam filters; furthermore, everyone on my list chose to be there, so I'm not spamming by purchasing lists of strangers and blasting e-mails out to them. Because of all this, my IP address is clean and appears on no spam blacklists.

On the other hand, with a hosted e-mail service, you're sharing a single server and IP address with hundreds or even thousands of other marketers, many of whom are potentially sending out lots of spammy content that gets the server IP address blocked all over the place—that's right, another filter. The bigger change, though, came from having total control of my mail server. I was no longer forced to use double opt-in and was finally free to test both and measure results. The clear winner was single opt-in, and it more than doubled my sales.

Not only does single opt-in work far better for me than double, but also I've noticed a lot of big-name marketers moving back to single recently. Here are some of the problems with double opt-in:

- No instant gratification. When people sign up to get your free download, report, or whatever else, they want it now. They don't want to be bothered with finding a verification link, clicking on it, waiting for another e-mail, and then finally getting the download link. After all that insanity, many people simply leave and find a competitor's site.

- Double opt-in only reminds people that they're joining a newsletter, and even though we're not spammers (you're really not, I hope), they are wary of getting more and more e-mail. So, after being dragged through that process, they'll go ahead and unsubscribe after they get your free download.

- Many people never receive the verification e-mail. Verification e-mails are increasingly winding up in spam folders. A lot of people can't be bothered to check their spam folder for the e-mail and, furthermore, getting your e-mail labeled as spam will reduce their confidence in you. They may conclude that you really are a spammer after all! Why else would your e-mail land there?

So, for me, single opt-in is my only choice. Like I said, test both. Maybe some people in odd markets do better with double, so you never know until you try both.

One last hint before I close out this chapter: Spam complaints are the bane of any e-mail marketer. Spam complaints will not only land your e-mail server on IP address blacklists, seriously hurting your deliverability, but can also get your hosting account shut down. Hosting companies hate spam complaints.

One smart way around this is to set up your e-mail software so when a customer clicks on an unsubscribe link, they are taken to a page that not only verifies their removal from the list, but also features a "Would you like to report this e-mail as spam?" mechanism, with yes and no options. This will drastically reduce the number of spam complaints you receive, maybe even down to zero, since the subscribers got their chance to vent and probably won't send a complaint to your hosting company at that point.

I won't give you any server, software, or service provider e-mails here; those things are constantly changing, so for a current list of my recommendations, go to NeverColdCallBook.com.

34

Up-Sells, Cross-Sells, and Down-Sells: Instant 50 Percent Sales Increase

A while back, I had created a fantastic new product, one that I'd put a lot of research, time, and effort into. I was very happy with the outcome.

That's the good news. The bad news is that it wasn't selling.

The first problem is that I hadn't done a product launch. Bad move on my part. The other problem is that I couldn't find an effective way to add it to my autoresponder series. A few people bought it, but it wasn't bringing in the killing I expected.

Then I learned about up-sells. Up-sells are equivalent to the proverbial "Would you like fries with that?"

Good marketers not only offer an up-sell but make it a very special offer that's available then, and then only. A one-time offer (OTO).

Instead of letting my new product continue twisting in the wind, I created a one-time offer page. What happened is that people would purchase my front-end product—the one the web site revolved around—and as soon as their purchase was complete, they were presented with a page that said, "Before continuing, please read this entire page. It's *that* important—you're never going to see it again."

My new and excited customer then saw a thank-you note from me, followed by a brief story of how the product came to be, the challenges I faced after perfecting the methods taught within, and then how I solved those problems to reach the top of the sales game.

Are you beginning to catch on yet?

Yes, this led right into an offer to buy that new product. But not just any offer—if the customer were to purchase right now, and only right now, they'd get the product at half price, and even be able to try it out free for 30 days.

If they left the page without buying, they'd never see that offer again and would be forced to pay full price.

And believe me, my systems are set up so nobody will ever see the offer again!

As a result of this, instead of maybe one in ten people buying the product down the road (if they didn't forget about it), sales immediately went up to one in three.

With some good copywriting and testing on the page, including a video of myself presenting the product, the conversion rate jumped to nearly half—yes, nearly half of the people who buy the front-end product bought the up-sell.

More recently, I added one-click technology to my shopping cart, meaning that customers can add the additional product with just one click of the mouse, rather than entering their billing information all over again. This has brought the conversion rate to 75 percent, or three out of four!

Not to change the subject, but this is a classic example of why the common thinking of "get more traffic, get more traffic" is largely a big distraction. The goal isn't necessarily to get more traffic—it's to increase your profits from the traffic *you already have!* In fact, I make it a rule to do some more optimizing and testing on a site *before* implementing any new traffic generation strategies, particularly if those strategies will cost me money. It's not only good business sense to squeeze every penny possible from your traffic stream, but it keeps me continually thinking and working on increasing my conversion rate, and, for me, that's not work. It's a fun hobby. It's like a game of chess, constantly anticipating a person's next move and beating him to it.

People respond to one-time offers because, first of all, they're already in a buying mode—they just bought from you a minute ago—and because there's value in taking advantage of the offer, especially since it's related to your front-end product, and your new customer is obviously in a buying mode in that area.

With a one-time offer, you must be firm and stand your ground. When an offer says, "Right now, and only right now—you'll never see it again," you have to mean it. Don't be one of those marketers who presents a one-time offer, then offers it over and over again. When you stand firm on your one-time offers, what happens is that your list becomes trained to respond to them. They've learned the hard way that Frank means business—if he says you'll never see an offer again, he means it!

On my sites, I use a PHP script (that's Internet marketing talk for software running on a web server) that records not only the customer's IP address and ISP hostname, but also cookies their browser. This gives three-way protection against the person ever seeing that offer again. Weaker one-time offer scripts might only cookie a browser (allowing the customer to simply delete it), or might only record an IP address. With the script I use, I get maximum protection against people accessing the offer again. (You can download the script for free at NeverColdCallBook.com.)

On that note, I never resend the offer to someone who asks for it a few days later. This is important, unless they have a really good reason such as their computer crashing in the middle of the purchase.

You don't have to have only one one-time offer. Lots of marketers will stack several, presenting more and more offers to the customer until he finally says no.

A cross-sell is different from an up-sell in that a cross-sell will recommend related products, without the urgency of an up-sell;

in other words, if you don't buy the cross-sell product(s) right then and there, they'll still be around for you to buy later.

The best example I can think of a cross-sell is Amazon.com, with their "Customers who purchased your book also purchased the following selections."

The nice thing about a cross-sell is that you don't even need to have additional products of your own to take advantage of this technique. A common way of adding easy additional income streams is to place an ad or link on your order confirmation page for products that you promote as an affiliate. For example, on the confirmation page for my Google AdWords training course, I suggest some products from Mike Filsaime, and I am paid commissions on those sales.

Finally, there is the down-sell. A down-sell is the practice of suggesting a lower-priced product to someone who declined to buy an up-sell (OTO) offer. You do this by offering a cheaper but related product, or perhaps a "lite" version of the OTO product.

An example might be me selling a four-disc DVD sales training package. If someone declines to buy the full package on the OTO, I can redirect them to a page that might offer only the first two DVDs for half the price of the OTO offer, with the stipulation that they may come back and purchase the second two DVDs later on if they'd like.

One rarely used method is the limited-time offer (LTO). A limited-time offer is exactly what it says: This special offer is available to you, but after a limited time, it will go away and you'll never see it again. Limited-time offers are particularly effective with product launches, or with any promotion to reignite a product. My favorite part is that it has a countdown clock display showing the prospective customer just how much time he has left before the offer disappears (the server knows to display the correct time for each individual customer by logging their IP address, ISP hostname, and by placing a cookie on their browser, as with the OTO script).

For more examples, ideas, and that free OTO script download, see NeverColdCallBook.com.

35

ABANDONED
SHOPPING CARTS:
A HIDDEN
PROFIT CENTER

For every person who buys your product, several more will visit the checkout page but click back without ever buying.

Instead of losing these customers forever, why not covertly follow up with them? I'm using a script now that sends a prewritten and timed series of e-mails to customers who leave my shopping cart without buying, complete with a link back to their cart just as they left it, including the correct product(s) and quantities.

Abandoned shopping cart scripts capture that customer's information in a variety of ways. The first is to grab their name and e-mail address at the opt-in and place it into a cookie for the duration of the browser session. Then, when the customer hits the shopping cart, the information is added into a database, complete with the cart contents (if they add any, that is).

The other method is to use a two-page shopping cart, although I don't care for that one because anything longer than a simple one-page checkout is going to hurt sales; multiple-step shopping carts act as filters, causing people to change their minds before actually clicking that all-important order button.

The beauty of abandoned cart scripts is that anyone who went as far as the checkout page really wants your product. The person just has some reservations about buying it. Maybe she has been ripped off before by similar offers, or perhaps she's worried about what her spouse will say. Either way, when someone was that close to actually buying, you want a chance to recover that sale. Anyone who has worked in sales knows how badly you want to get back in front of a hot prospect after they send you the "no" e-mail.

Abandoned cart scripts accomplish this, and very well. Someone who was on the fence and got as far as the checkout page before backing off will frequently be swayed by a, "Hey, I noticed you were almost going to buy, but didn't, what are your concerns?" e-mail.

If that and the next couple of follow-ups don't work, the last and final one saying, "Your cart contents are about to expire, you'd better go check out now while you still can" frequently does the trick.

Like I said in the previous chapter, maximizing profits from your existing traffic is more important than endlessly trying to get more traffic.

Abandoned cart scripts are much like autoresponders. An autoresponder is there to generate interest and get people who were mildly interested at first to buy. Abandoned cart scripts take people who are on the fence and push them over to the buy side.

Abandoned cart scripts are rare, but for an up-to-date listing of where you can find them, see NeverColdCallBook.com.

36

ONLINE CONVERSION TESTING TO EXPLODE YOUR PROFITS

Once you've gotten all of your marketing systems and techniques up and running, you need to find out which ones are working and which aren't, and precisely how many unique visitors, opt-ins, sales, up-sells, and so on, each one is generating. These different items and the statistics that go with them are known as metrics.

Why? Because the secret to Internet marketing greatness is testing and measuring.

When you know exactly what kind of results each traffic source is getting you, you can make adjustments accordingly. You back off on the ones that aren't working, and you crank up the ones that are.

This is particularly true with PPC marketing. If I'm spending $200/month on a keyword that's only getting $180 in sales, it's time to reduce the bid price for that keyword. On the other hand, if I have a keyword that costs the same $200/month and is bringing in $2,000 in sales, you bet I'm going to crank up the spending on that one.

With free traffic sources, there are tons of things to keep track of. You can see trends and adjust your strategies accordingly. You can discover sneaky new ways of bringing in quality traffic with social media.

More importantly, you can abandon free traffic sources that don't bring in sales. They're not worth wasting your time on, and they're not worth paying someone to run.

In addition to measuring traffic metrics, you need to test and measure what's working on your site, all of the different pages— including your landing page, sales page, up-sell/cross-sell/ down-sell pages, and much more.

For me, this testing and measuring never ends. You may think that NeverColdCall.com, at almost seven years old, is perfect.

It's not—far from it!

In fact, as I'm sitting here writing this, I have a test running on my sales page. It takes six items on the page and tests three different combinations of text and graphics for each one, plus six total variations on the page headline, for a total of—hang on to your hat—4,374 possible combinations!

Over a period of a few weeks, the software tracks the results for each and every combination, and once statistical significance is reached (the point where enough testing has been done to declare a clear winner), it goes a step further and tests only the winning combination against my original, or static, page.

This kind of test, known as a multivariate or Taguchi test, named after the Japanese mathematician who invented it, is one of the most powerful weapons a great marketer has at his or her disposal.

Here are the most common tests you'll want to employ to become a truly great marketer.

- General traffic and conversion testing. This simply refers to measuring all of your incoming traffic, determining the source, and learning what gets results and what doesn't. A free tracking suite is available from Google Analytics, although it does have limitations and I'd recommend a paid software package instead—look for recommendations at NeverColdCallBook.com.

- Google AdWords tracking. Again, AdWords itself offers a free conversion traffic package, simply called AdWords Conversion Tracking, but like Google Analytics, it has limitations and shortcomings and I'd look for a paid alternative instead (great ones are available starting at around $30/month).
- A/B and A/B/C split-testing. What this does is let you create two or three pages that are alternatives to the static page, and it distributes incoming traffic equally among them. It then tracks conversions, including opt-ins, sales, and more, and after enough traffic has passed through to declare a clear winner, you'll know which page works best.
- Multivariate, or Taguchi, testing. This is the most advanced form of web site testing, and the one I now use. I used A/B split-testing for years, but the problem is that it's too slow. Multivariate testing, on the other hand, is a much faster version of split-testing because you can, in the case of the software I'm using, test up to seven different variables on a page simultaneously, for a total of 4,374 combinations. So, in the time it would take to complete just one A/B split-test, you're effectively doing thousands. It exponentially increases your results because it covers so much more ground in such a short time.

Remember, testing and measuring are everything in marketing. Everything! If you don't know what's working and what's not, you are in the dark and you have no way of improving your results with time.

For far more in-depth information on testing, as well as specific software recommendations, including the ones I use myself, see NeverColdCallBook.com.

Part VI

UNLOCK HIDDEN BACK-END PROFITS

37

BACK-END PROFITS: INTERNET MARKETING'S BIGGEST PRIZE

After I'd established myself as a top marketer, built a solid business platform, and really started making big money, I had a huge eye-opening experience: That was only the beginning!

Selling my front-end product is great, but as more people buy it, word-of-mouth spreads, and my list continues to grow, the potential to make money on the back-end has reached a tipping point where it's even more profitable than selling my front-end products.

How can this be?

It's easy: Every salesperson, or anyone involved in business at any level, knows that it's easier to profit from an existing customer than it is to go out and earn a new one. There are no sales or marketing costs involved. These present customers already know who you are and know that you deliver as promised. They've already bought from you, and, as a result, are predisposed to you again because most people are loyal and are comfortable with familiarity.

There is a common trap that Internet marketers fall into, and that's the trap of continually obsessing over selling more of their front-end product.

Now, don't get me wrong here. It's a good idea to maximize the sales on your front-end product. I continue to do so. The problems arise when marketers spend *all* of their productive time working on that.

Again, it's easier to profit from existing customers and subscribers than it is to get new ones. So, once your front-end sales have reached a level you're happy with (though many marketers are never satisfied), begin looking for back-end profits.

Here are some examples of how to do that.

- Back-end products. This one is a no-brainer. Create more products that your customers would want to buy. You can even include one or more as up-sells immediately following the front-end product purchase, or you can launch them later on.
- Intangible services. These include paid speaking, coaching, and consulting. Once you've established yourself as an authority figure per the steps in Part II of the book, this income starts rolling in fairly easily, and you'll probably even get requests for it without having to actively promote.
- Affiliate income. This is my personal favorite. I routinely earn five-figure checks just for sending out one e-mail to my list—one! The key here is to make sure you're only promoting high-quality products from high-quality people—if you promote junk or scams, you'll lose your list and your reputation very quickly.
- Post-sale marketing. This is related to affiliate marketing, but instead of sending e-mails out to your list, or posting affiliate links on your blog, you strategically place an ad on your order confirmation, or thank-you page, for a related product that earns you commissions on sales. This is otherwise known as a cross-sell, but instead of cross-selling your own product, you're doing it as an affiliate for someone else.

- Membership sites. I love membership sites! People join, sign up to pay a monthly, automatic recurring fee, and that gives them access to high-quality content, forums, and more. The challenge here is keeping the site up to date—if you get lazy and fail to add great new content every month, along with value-adds like teleseminars and webinars, your subscribers will cancel quickly.
- Continuity products. These are products that automatically ship to you, each month, and you are automatically charged for them. Book clubs are a great example. My *Sales Pro Secrets* course that opens periodically is another. These are harder to maintain because shipping a physical product is involved, but many reputable fulfillment houses can handle this competently, including making sure each individual member receives the appropriate month's content each month, per their membership. Again, the big challenge here is coming up with enough new material, and on time, factoring in production and replication delays. The best way to begin a physical continuity product is to have several months' work already completed and mastered by your replication company so they're ready to produce more on a moment's notice.

Those are just a few methods of monetizing your list. Remember, it's easier to sell to existing customers than to market to new ones, so don't overlook the tremendous asset you have in your list.

38

MONETIZE YOUR LIST WITH AFFILIATE PROMOTIONS

As I mentioned in the previous chapter, promoting for others as an affiliate is a very easy way to make potentially big money, with little or no work on your part.

The secret to succeeding with it is, first, to have a solid business platform.

Many people who first discover Internet marketing buy into the myth that you can make a fortune without your own product or business. They buy into the snake-oil salesman who claims that you can get started immediately and make a killing with little or no effort.

The problem here is that while it's theoretically possible to do this (it rarely happens in reality), even if you can earn some money this way, you'll never make anything substantial.

The reasons are quite simple. First of all, the key to affiliate income for me, at least, is my list. I've built a large and loyal list by using exactly the techniques laid out in this book.

Second, if you want to make big money as an affiliate, you need to have a recognizable name—a brand, if you will—in order to put forth enough authority and gain enough trust from people for them to follow your recommendations and click on your affiliate link (and buy).

Finally, when there is so much money to be made on this vast thing called the Internet, why on earth would you limit yourself by trying to strictly promote to others instead of building your own business? As Robert Kiyosaki likes to say, the best investment isn't found in stock markets or real estate. The best investment in the world is your own business.

So, if you bought this book and skipped straight to this chapter, looking for get-rich-quick advice on affiliate promotions, I'm sorry to tell you, it ain't here. You'll need to go back, start from the beginning, and build a platform, a brand, and a business before you can expect to make five figures with a single e-mail as I do today.

With that out of the way, what to promote?

The fastest and easiest way to find products to promote to your list is through affiliate networks, such as PayDotCom.com and ClickBank.com. These are web sites that feature products available for sale through affiliate programs. You can sign up as a member and find products you can promote to others, as well as submit your own product to the directory so others can promote it for you. These sites are an extremely simple way to get started with affiliate promotions.

The next method is to look for products that are in, or related to, your niche or industry. You may already know of some that would go over well with your audience, and you can also search the Web for more and look for each marketer's affiliate program.

The next way is through joint ventures. As you succeed online, even if you are selling into an offline industry and are not in the Internet marketing niche per se, you will be discovered by the Internet marketing community, because the most successful marketers tend to be the ones selling real-world offline products. As you gain a following there, you'll be offered joint venture opportunities all the time, complete with affiliate programs. Eventually the joint venture requests will become overwhelming, as is the case for me, and you'll find yourself refusing most and only promoting for a core group of very reputable people, like I do today.

Another way is through multilevel, or direct marketing, companies. Make sure you find a reputable one, because many aren't, and make sure its product or service is relevant to your subscribers. If you can find one that meets these criteria, it's a fantastic way to generate an income stream that is not only easy and automatic, but always growing as well.

Finally, you can ask around. As you meet other Internet marketers, and you should, at seminars and other gatherings, ask people who make good money as affiliates what they're promoting. You want to make sure the products you choose to promote aren't just high-quality, but also sell. Don't pick the next Edsel and wonder why no commission checks ever appear in your mailbox.

I have a couple of core rules I follow hard and fast when it comes to doing affiliate promotions.

- Don't promote too frequently. I restrict mine to no more than a couple per month. The reason is twofold. One, if you send out affiliate promotions too often, people will get tired of them and unsubscribe from your list. Two, people joined your list to get quality content from you. You build loyalty with your list by providing that great content and in return, your subscribers will value your opinions and will appreciate your recommendations for third-party products. You can only be an effective affiliate marketer when you have the trust and respect of your list, and you don't earn that by continually pummeling them with promotions.
- I don't promote to brand-new subscribers. When people join my list, they're obviously a hot prospect and pretty close to buying my front-end product. I don't want to distract them with affiliate promotions, and I'm also trying to earn their respect, trust, and loyalty as this stage. So, I only send affiliate promotions to subscribers who have been on my list for at least 60 days (my e-mail software allows me to segment lists like that). That way, I'm not distracting people who may be on the brink of buying my own product and I'm not risking losing them right away, since a brand-new subscriber doesn't know

me yet and may just assume my newsletter is just another one of those that exist solely to blast out affiliate promotions.

- In addition to sending broadcast e-mails out to my list, when I find a product or program that sells extremely well and that brings me a lot of positive feedback, I make it a permanent fixture in my autoresponder series. I'll insert it far enough down that only subscribers who have been on-board for at least 60 days receive it. Doing this brings me consistent, recurring income every month without the need to actively promote.

For more information and resources on promoting as an affiliate, including complete home study courses on the subject, see NeverColdCallBook.com.

39

USE YOUR
ONLINE IDENTITY
TO GENERATE
OFFLINE INCOME

A big part of building a solid business platform is to be some-one; in other words, get yourself recognition, exposure, and, most importantly, expert credibility and authority.

Coaching, consulting, advisory positions, paid speaking, and so many more outlets are unlocked to you as soon as you brand yourself with the magic of expert status.

Here are the big ones.

- Coaching. This is the easiest place to start, if you are selling some type of information product, but with some creativity it is available to anyone doing business. It is easier to begin, though, if you do have a book or information product. People are constantly asking me for coaching, although I rarely offer one-on-one coaching because I don't have to—I have too many other high-income streams that require little or none of my time. However, for an up-and-coming marketer, this is a great source of substantial income. After a new customer buys your product, offer coaching sessions immediately following the sale, as an OTO up-sell, or offer it later on in follow-up communications. Be careful, though, that you don't tie up your entire schedule with coaching. Leave plenty of your time free to continually improve your marketing processes, learn, attend live events, and network with other marketers.

- Group coaching. This is similar to one-on-one coaching, with the exception that you have several people on each call. Obviously, you can't charge as much for this, but it may be a better alternative since it's easier to sell a lower-cost option, especially if you are not fully established yet, and because it covers much more ground in far less time, leaving your time free to improve your marketing.

- Hiring coaches. With this, you hire and train competent individuals on your product, and on coaching others on the relevant topics. This doesn't necessarily mean leasing an office and staffing it with employees—the better option is to get online, find qualified people who can do the job as independent contractors from home, and get them up to speed. Be sure to stay in contact with the clients, however, and get feedback to make sure your coaches are doing their jobs. Of course, you need to have a very solid brand, platform, and reputation before you can expect people to pay for your coaching program that is delivered by someone else.

- Outsourced coaching. This is how the big guys do it. There are dozens of companies in large offices that can take your product, devour it, and, with your help, transform it into a coaching program. They will then market it either to your list that you provide or, even better, they will actively market it through an advertising campaign at their own expense. (If you've ever heard all the ads for coaching programs on satellite radio, that's exactly what they are.) While these companies only pay you about 25 percent of gross receipts as your cut, that cut is frequently huge. Many top authors and marketers are earning hundreds of thousands of dollars per *month* this way!

- Consulting. This is a big one if you are in any niche related to business, be it big business, small business, online business, or entrepreneurship. It's only natural for people to read a book or information product and subsequently want to pay the author to personally come in and solve all their problems for them. It's very effective for clients because not only are they bringing in a qualified expert with extensive knowledge, but bringing in a fresh perspective with a clear head is powerful as well (I was recently paid $5,000 by a local company to sit in on their two-hour sales meeting because of competitive challenges they found impossible; together, with me facilitating, they figured it all out in about 30 minutes).

- Paid teleseminars or webinars. These are common in the sales niche that I'm in. Customers will pay $50 or $100 to call or log into a one- or two-hour teleseminar or webinar, listen to the presentation from the featured expert, and then participate in a Q&A session. It's particularly valuable and exciting for the participants to interact with someone they respect and follow, and it's hugely profitable for the host—dozens or even hundreds of people paying a hundred dollars each is a nice paycheck for a couple of hours work, and for me, I find them very enjoyable—not work at all—and I frequently learn something new myself from a participant.

- Paid speaking. This is where many experts make huge money. I know authors who are paid upwards of $25,000 for a 40-minute keynote speech, and they are doing several each month. On the entry-level side of the spectrum, you can be paid several hundred dollars per speech right away with just a web site and a product establishing your identity. With a few media credentials, articles, and even a small following, you can quickly get to the $1,000 or $2,000 range. Within a year or so, if you work diligently at building your online business and you network effectively, $5,000 isn't out of the question. Beyond that, you'll need to have a professional demo DVD made, so potential clients can watch an actual speech of yours before hiring you, and you'll also have to have serious media credentials and usually a published book as well.

- Platform selling. Platform selling, or "pitching," is when you are not paid any up-front speaking fees to speak, but instead promote a product to the audience and are paid a percentage of sales, typically 50 percent. Many larger speaking tours that fill major arenas with huge audiences may pay as little as 20 percent due to the size of the audience you're getting, as well as their production costs. While this is not my preferred method of speaking, primarily because it would contradict my previous books' themes of *not* actively selling, don't make the mistake of thinking that it's a "Plan B" for people who can't get paid speaking gigs. On the contrary, I know people who routinely make $30,000 or more per speech, and strongly prefer platform selling to paid speaking.

Those are just some of the possibilities available to you once you have begun building an online business platform. And while you may think they're only open to authors and information marketers, think again. If you own any kind of offline business, say, an HVAC contractor, the fact that you own a business and are doing it successfully will make people want your advice, and will quality you for all the above.

For a list of resources to help you get started in coaching, consulting, speaking, and more—including the name and contact information for my own personal speaking consultant—see NeverColdCallBook.com.

AFTERWORD:
THE POSSIBILITIES
ARE ENDLESS

Back in 2002, I was a small business owner.

And I was broke.

I was half-owner of a telecom and Internet services sales agency in Phoenix, Arizona.

We had been on top of the world, riding high, living the good life—and not saving any of our substantial income while doing so.

Then 9/11 hit, and our high incomes went down to almost nothing.

There were no more sales that September, following the eleventh.

There were no sales in October.

There were few sales the remainder of the year, and while things started to pick up in the spring, I was so deep in the hole that I had no choice but to go out and get a sales job with a high base salary. With my bank balance showing a whopping $18, what else could I do?

And while it was nice to pay the bills again and go out to dinner once in a while, I hated returning to a job after enjoying the relative freedom that owning your own business provides.

Sure, it took up a lot of my time, and I even made a lot of the sales myself (my partner ran the technical side), but still, the business was mine.

If you own a small business, or have in the past, you can certainly understand how painful it was to go back to working for someone else.

Even though I hated working at a job, I was consistently the top sales rep in my new employer's branch, shocking all the other sales reps at how quickly I rose to the top.

They soon began asking me questions.

Lots of them.

They wanted to learn my secrets.

At this point the light bulb went off in my head. I realized that if people were so desperate to gain my sales knowledge, there must be a market for it—in other words, people would probably be willing to pay for it!

Over the following weekend, which I remember very well—I went from Friday afternoon through Sunday evening without any sleep—I put all of my sales knowledge and secrets on paper. That week I went to a computer store, bought a microphone and recording software, and created two CDs to accompany the workbook.

I put up a web site (a very poor one, since I knew nothing at the time), I paid $5 to sign up for Google AdWords, and created my first—and very crude—campaign in about an hour, and I turned it live.

Thirty minutes later, I had my first sale.

Sales continued to trickle in, gaining momentum, until I quit that job—my last job ever—a short six weeks later.

Then I became a student of Internet marketing. I learned the basics, like adding an e-mail list and opt-in form to my site's home page, something I didn't even have for about the first three months.

My success began to compound as I continued to learn and apply more and more knowledge of Internet marketing.

Less than a year later, I walked into the local Mercedes-Benz dealership and wrote a check for my dream car, a beautiful black S500.

I began racking up interviews and other media coverage—even before I learned the media techniques presented in this book.

Later that same year, major New York publishers came ringing, which eventually resulted in my first published book. Due to an Internet launch exactly like I've described in the chapter on product launches in this book, and with the aid of several joint venture partners, the book shot to #1 on Amazon within three hours of pushing the launch button, and it made the *New York Times* business best-seller list that month.

And from there, the good things continued, right through to today.

In fact, that very first product, the one that freed me from my last job almost seven years ago, *Cold Calling Is a Waste of Time: Sales Success in the Information Age*, continues, after several revisions, to be my top-selling product. And sales continue to rise.

You'd think they'd trail off after so long, but not when the marketer behind the book continues to learn and improve.

What will Internet marketing do for you?

If you're a salesperson looking for a new way to generate hot leads without prospecting, you've found the right book to teach you how.

If you're a business owner, either large or small, wanting to multiply your sales and profits, Internet marketing will do that for you.

If you are an eager entrepreneur who wants to become a multi-millionaire, welcome home. Internet marketing is the place for you; in fact, I know several marketers who started with nothing and are already millionaires—while still in their twenties!

Remember, you can achieve any financial goal with Internet marketing. All it takes is the desire and the commitment to get you there—all of the tools have been provided for you. I've shown you the basics in this book, enough to get you started and making money right away, as I did when I first started out.

I wish you the best of luck in your online journey. It may take time and commitment, but truly, making money online is relatively easy. The Internet gives us powers never seen before in the world of marketing. Use them!

I'd love to hear your thoughts, comments, feedback, and questions. Feel free to e-mail me at frank@NeverColdCallBook.com.

Appendix

A PRIMER ON INTEGRATION MARKETING

Mark Joyner
#1 Best-selling Author of Integration Marketing *and many other books . . .*

I'd like to thank Frank for asking me to write this primer for his readers.

Ever since I coined the phrase "Integration Marketing" in the 90s, it has caused a great deal of discussion, but also a fair bit of confusion. The way I taught it to many of my earlier students of the discipline led them to believe that a single marketing tactic (for example, the integration of an offer on someone's thank-you page) was the be-all-end-all of Integration Marketing. That's a little misguided, but as their teacher I take full responsibility and am glad to have the chance to set the record straight.

Those of you who have read the book *Integration Marketing* (John Wiley & Sons, 2009) realize that marketing tactic is only a drop in one rather large (and potentially hugely profitable) bucket. As you know, that book is a short and easy read, but it gets into more detail than I can go into here. The extra detail in the book is necessary. I won't tell you that I can do justice to the topic in a short primer; however, I'll do my best.

The best I can hope for is that you'll dig into this topic more deeply—not just for further study but for further application. The application of these ideas is what will make you rich—as they did for Microsoft, McDonald's, a few hip-hop artists, and many others.

First, here is the formal definition of Integration Marketing as I outlined in the book:

Integration Marketing: The integration of a (UMV) "Unit of Marketing Value" (a brand message, an offer, a sale, a store—anything that adds marketing impact to your business) into an existing "Integration Point" (inside a "Traffic Stream" or "Transaction Stream").

That's a small statement, but it packs a lot of wallop.

Let's start with some of the smaller ideas.

First, you can integrate your own "UMVs" into your own marketing processes.

For example, if someone purchases something on your web page, you can then offer him or her an additional product to purchase on your thank-you page.

That alone can double your profits.

Do the same thing on the thank-you page of someone else's web site and that can bring in money out of thin air.

Next, do this as a strategic principle of growth for your company and you can not only bring in a steady stream of profit, but you can do so with very little risk. (Hint: Most Integration Marketing has almost zero risk.)

This may sound unremarkable until you discover that it's the exact same strategy that shot Microsoft into the stratosphere. They simply integrated their product (DOS) into someone else's Transaction Stream (IBM) and then used that same deal as a strategic growth principle.

The same can be said of McDonald's.

And of U.S. Steel.

And countless other titans of industry.

If you think that business growth can't be that simple, you're not alone. Most of us tend to overcomplicate things and that's part of the problem. When we're staring a simple method for massive growth in the face we want to be repeatedly congratulated on our creativity so we are forced to innovate again and again—sometimes to our demise.

So, sit back and embrace the simple. Microsoft did.

There's a lot more that can be said about Integration Marketing (hence the whole book on the topic), but I'll give you a little clue as to how pervasive it is. See, it's right under your nose all the time and you don't even catch it.

It's happening right now, for example. Did you catch it? If not, ask a friend and make a game of solving this riddle.

Oh, there, it happened again.

INDEX